Quick & Simple
cooking

THE AUSTRALIAN
Women's Weekly

contents

We got the idea for this book almost out of necessity. Not everyone can manage a well thought out weekly shopping list, and who wants to stop at the supermarket on the way home from a long day at work? We've developed a list of pantry, refrigerator and freezer staples that can be magically brought to life as fresh, nutritious meals for those days you've had a million things to think about other than dinner. See the shopping list on the following pages and stock your kitchen with the ingredients you need to 'cook from the pantry'. Of course, no meal is complete without dessert – at least it's not in my house; so we also have a whole chapter devoted to sweet endings made with on-hand ingredients.

Pamela Clark
Food Director

kitchen staples

PANTRY

Canned goods
bamboo shoots
beans, kidney
beans, white
brown lentils
chickpeas
milk, coconut
milk, light coconut
passionfruit in syrup
pink salmon
sour cherries in syrup
tuna in oil
tuna in springwater
whole baby beetroot
whole tomatoes

Spices
allspice
bay leaves
caraway seeds
cayenne pepper
chilli flakes
chilli powder
cinnamon stick
dried curry leaves
garam masala
ground cardamom
ground cinnamon
ground clove
ground coriander
ground cumin
ground ginger
ground nutmeg
pepper medley
smoked paprika
sumac

Stocks
beef
chicken
fish
vegetable

Pastas, rices and other grains
breads
   flour tortillas
   lebanese flatbread
   wholemeal bread
grains
   couscous
   pearl barley
   polenta
noodles
   egg noodles
   rice vermicelli
pasta
   angel hair
   fettuccine
   penne
   risoni
   spaghetti
peas
   chickpeas
   yellow split peas
rice
   arborio
   basmati
   brown long-grain
   jasmine
   white long-grain

Fresh fruit and vegetables
apples
carrots
corella pears
garlic
kumara
lemon
lime
onions
   brown
   red
oranges
potatoes
pumpkin
   butternut
   jap
tomatoes
   cherry
   grape

Vinegars, sauces, and oils (liquid basics)
coconut essence
honey
oil
   olive
   peanut
   sesame
   vegetable
port
sauces
   hoisin
   light soy
   oyster
   Tabasco
syrup
   light corn
   maple
tomato paste
vanilla extract
vinegar
   apple cider
   balsamic
   red wine
   white
   white wine
wine
   chinese cooking
   dry white
   white

Being organised in the kitchen means never being without an ingredient, and therefore a meal. With this comprehensive list of food for the pantry, freezer and refrigerator, you'll never have a dinner dilemma again.

Pantry basics (dry basics)

bicarbonate of soda
breadcrumbs, packaged
chocolate
 dark and milk eating
chunky tomato salsa
coconut
 dessicated
 shredded
cornichons
dried cranberries
flour
 plain
 self-raising
nuts
 almond meal
 almonds
 roasted almonds
 pecans
 pine nuts
 roasted pine nuts
 roasted unsalted
  peanuts
 walnuts
pappadams
peanut butter
raisins
salt
 sea salt
 table salt
sugar
 brown
 caster
 icing
 white

REFRIGERATOR

Dairy

butter
buttermilk
cheese
 cheddar
 fetta
 firm ricotta
 haloumi
 mascarpone
 parmesan
 ricotta
cream
 single
 sour
 thickened
milk
yogurt
 greek-style
 plain

Fresh food

capsicum, red
celery
eggs
lebanese cucumber
mushrooms
 button
 oyster
 shiitake
 swiss brown
olives, seeded kalamata
savoy cabbage
shallots

Meat, poultry, fish

bacon
 rindless rashers
 rindless streaky
beef
 mince
 rib-eye steaks
 thin sausages
chicken
 breast fillets
 skinless thigh fillets
 whole (2kg)
fish
 anchovy fillets
 firm white fillets
 ocean trout
 smoked salmon
ham, sliced leg
lamb
 fillets
 merguez sausages
 loin chops
 mince
pork
 cutlets
 sausages
 smoked chorizo
  sausages
veal schnitzel

Fresh herbs

coriander leaves
dill
flat-leaf parsley leaves
ginger
mint leaves
rosemary
sage leaves

Sauces, pastes, mustards, etc

basil pesto
curry pastes
 red
 tikka masala (or
  your favourite)
horseradish, prepared
mayonnaise
mustard
 dijon
 english
 wholegrain
preserved lemon
sambal oelek
sauces
 fish
 kecap manis
 worcestershire

Jarred goods

baby capers
capers
capsicum strips
jarred jalapeno chillies
marinated artichokes

FREEZER

Frozen fruit and vegetables

broad beans
corn kernals
mixed berries
peas
spinach

Meat, poultry, fish

beef
 mince
 rib-eye steaks
chicken
 breast fillets
 thigh fillets
 whole (2kg)
fish
 firm white fillets
lamb
 fillets
 loin chops
pork
 cutlets
veal
 schnitzel

Other

335g pizza bases
pastry, ready-rolled
 fillo
 puff pastry
 shortcrust pastry

the indispensable egg

The ultimate fast food, the humble egg is a little package of goodness that cooks in minutes and adds richness and flavour to so many recipes. They are a meal on their own and an indispensable part of many others. Packed with protein, and with the healthy heart tick from the Heart Foundation, they are also part of a balanced diet. Eggs last for 4 weeks when kept in the refrigerator, so have a carton handy and you'll always have dinner ready without a trip to the shops.

tortilla de patata

[**preparation time** 10 minutes **cooking time** 30 minutes **serves** 4]

20g butter
¼ cup (60ml) olive oil
3 medium potatoes (600g), chopped finely
1 medium brown onion (150g), chopped finely
8 eggs
½ teaspoon chilli powder

1 Preheat oven to 180°C/160°C fan-forced.
2 Melt butter with oil in 22cm-base ovenproof frying pan; cook potato and onion, stirring occasionally, until potato is tender.
3 Meanwhile, whisk eggs and chilli powder in medium jug.
4 Add egg mixture to pan. Cook, uncovered, over low heat, about 5 minutes or until just set.
5 Place pan in oven; cook, uncovered, about 10 minutes or until browned lightly. Carefully turn tortilla onto plate. Cut into wedges; serve with a side salad.
nutritional count per serving **28.4g total fat (7.8g saturated fat); 1747kJ (418 cal); 22g carbohydrate; 17.5g protein; 28.4g fibre**

[**preparation time** 20 minutes **cooking time** 40 minutes **serves** 4]

eggs gado gado

1 medium potato (200g), sliced thinly
1 medium carrot (120g), sliced thinly
2 cups (160g) finely shredded cabbage
¾ cup (90g) frozen peas
1 lebanese cucumber (130g), sliced thinly
6 hard-boiled eggs, quartered
peanut dressing
¼ cup (70g) crunchy peanut butter
1 tablespoon light soy sauce
2 teaspoons brown sugar
1 tablespoon lime juice
¼ cup (60ml) light coconut milk

You need approximately a quarter of a small savoy cabbage for this recipe. This traditional Indonesian vegetable salad is a great snack to include in kids' lunchboxes.
Fried firm tofu, can be included in gado gado, making this a perfectly substantial meal for vegetarians, too.

1 Place potato in baking-paper-lined bamboo steamer. Steam, covered, over wok of simmering water for 3 minutes. Add carrot; steam, covered, for 2 minutes. Add cabbage and peas; steam, covered, about 2 minutes or until vegetables are tender.
2 Meanwhile, make peanut dressing.
3 Place vegetables in bowl with cucumber; top with egg. Drizzle with dressing. Serve with lime wedges and coriander, if you like.
peanut dressing Stir ingredients in small saucepan over low heat until mixture combines. Remove from heat; stir in about 1 tablespoon of water.
nutritional count per serving **18.9g total fat (5.6g saturated fat); 1342kJ (321 cal); 15.8g carbohydrate; 18.9g protein; 6.8g fibre**

4 egg yolks
¾ cup (60g) finely grated parmesan cheese
4 rindless bacon rashers (260g), chopped finely
2 cloves garlic, sliced thinly
1 cup (120g) frozen peas
375g spaghetti

1   Combine egg yolks and cheese in small bowl.
2   Cook bacon over heat in medium frying pan about 5 minutes or until starting to crisp. Add garlic; cook, stirring, 1 minute. Add peas; cook, stirring, until heated through.
3   Meanwhile, cook pasta, uncovered, in large saucepan of boiling water until tender; drain, reserving ¼ cup cooking liquid.
4   Return pasta to saucepan. Add bacon mixture, egg mixture and reserved cooking liquid to pasta; stir over heat about 1 minute.
5   Serve with extra parmesan cheese, if you like.
nutritional count per serving **15.3g total fat (6.3g saturated fat); 2332kJ (558 cal); 66.8g carbohydrate; 35g protein; 5.1g fibre**

spaghetti carbonara with peas

Unlike the cream-laden carbonara that many of us are familiar with, traditional carbonara is not made with any cream. We've slightly altered the traditional carbonara recipe by adding peas; if you prefer your pasta pea-free, simply omit them from the recipe.

[**preparation time** 15 minutes **cooking time** 10 minutes **serves** 4]

Serve the bake with a baby spinach and cherry tomato salad for a fuss-free dinner solution.

[**preparation time** 15 minutes **cooking time** 45 minutes **serves** 4]

kumara, bacon and egg bake

1 large kumara (500g), sliced thinly
1½ teaspoons ground cumin
5 rindless bacon rashers (325g), chopped finely
1 medium brown onion (150g), chopped finely
8 eggs
¼ cup (60ml) cream
1 cup (120g) coarsely grated cheddar cheese

1　Preheat oven to 180°C/160°C fan-forced. Grease 2.5 litre (10-cup) baking dish.
2　Boil, steam or microwave kumara 5 minutes. Drain; pat dry with absorbent paper. Place in single layer over base of dish; sprinkle with ½ teaspoon of the cumin.
3　Meanwhile, cook bacon and onion over heat in medium frying pan about 5 minutes or until onion softens. Stir in remaining cumin, spread mixture over kumara.
4　Whisk eggs, cream and cheese in medium bowl; pour over kumara mixture. Bake, uncovered, in oven, 30 minutes.

nutritional count per serving **31.7g total fat (15.6g saturated fat); 2195kJ (525 cal); 18.1g carbohydrate; 41.1g protein; 2.4g fibre**

[**preparation time** 25 minutes (plus refrigeration time) **cooking time** 35 minutes **serves** 4]

poached egg on grilled polenta with capsicum olive relish

2 cups (500ml) water
½ cup (85g) polenta
½ cup (40g) coarsely grated parmesan cheese
20g butter
4 eggs
capsicum olive relish
1 tablespoon olive oil
1 small red onion (100g), chopped finely
2 cloves garlic, sliced thinly
400g can crushed tomatoes
¼ cup (60ml) balsamic vinegar
1 tablespoon caster sugar
1 tablespoon water
½ cup (100g) roasted capsicum strips
⅓ cup (55g) seeded black olives, halved
⅓ cup loosely packed fresh flat-leaf parsley leaves

1 Oil a deep 19cm-square cake pan.
2 Bring the water to the boil in a large saucepan. Gradually stir polenta into the water; reduce heat, simmer, stirring, about 5 minutes or until polenta thickens. Stir in cheese and half the butter. Spread polenta into pan; cool 10 minutes. Cover; refrigerate about 45 minutes or until polenta is firm.
3 Meanwhile, make capsicum olive relish.
4 Preheat grill.
5 Melt remaining butter. Cut polenta into 4 squares; brush with melted butter. Grill about 5 minutes or until browned lightly.
6 Half-fill a medium frying pan with water; bring to the boil. Break one egg into a cup; slide into pan. Repeat with remaining eggs; when all eggs are in the pan, return the water to the boil. Cover pan, turn off heat; stand about 4 minutes or until eggs are set. Remove eggs, one at a time, using a slotted spoon; place spoon on absorbent-paper-lined saucer briefly to blot up any poaching liquid.
7 Spoon capsicum olive relish over polenta; top with egg.
capsicum olive relish Heat oil in medium frying pan; cook onion and garlic, stirring, until onion softens. Stir in undrained tomatoes. Add vinegar, sugar, the water, capsicum and olives; cook, uncovered, about 15 minutes or until mixture has thickened. Stir in parsley.
nutritional count per serving **19.7g total fat (7.3g saturated fat); 1455kJ (348 cal); 27.4g carbohydrate; 14g protein; 2.8g fibre**

Roasted capsicum strips are available from supermarkets and delicatessens. If you have a glut of red capsicums, you can always roast your own, slice thinly and keep, refrigerated, covered with olive oil, in a jar – they are a great addition to salads, pizzas and toasted sandwiches.

Low-in-fat, gluten-free and delicious, this soup is a perfect afternoon pick-me-up; double the recipe and freeze leftover portions to take to work.

[**preparation time** 10 minutes **cooking time** 20 minutes **serves** 4]

egg drop soup

1 litre (4 cups) water
1 litre (4 cups) chicken stock
1 tablespoon light soy sauce
1 tablespoon chinese cooking wine
1 clove garlic, crushed
5cm piece fresh ginger (25g), grated
400g chicken breast fillets
3 eggs, beaten lightly
125g rice vermicelli, soaked, drained
¼ cup loosely packed fresh coriander leaves
1 green onion, cut diagonally
2 tablespoons coarsely chopped unsalted
    roasted peanuts

1   Bring the water, stock, sauce, wine, garlic and ginger to the boil in large saucepan; add chicken, return to the boil. Reduce heat; simmer, covered, about 10 minutes or until chicken is cooked. Remove chicken; using two forks, shred meat.
2   Gradually whisk egg into the broth in a steady stream. Return chicken to pan.
3   Divide noodles among serving bowls; ladle soup into bowls, then sprinkle with coriander, onion and peanuts.
nutritional count per serving **15.1g total fat (4.1g saturated fat); 1551kJ (371 cal); 24.2g carbohydrate; 33.1g protein; 1.4g fibre**

8 slices wholemeal bread (360g)
8 slices leg ham (240g)
40g butter
4 eggs
cheese béchamel
20g butter
1 tablespoon plain flour
¾ cup (180ml) milk
½ cup (60g) finely grated cheddar cheese
1 tablespoon finely chopped fresh flat-leaf parsley

1   Make cheese béchamel.
2   Spread béchamel onto bread slices. Top four slices with ham then remaining bread.
3   Melt butter in large frying pan. Add sandwiches; toast, in batches, until browned both sides.
4   Fry eggs in same pan until cooked. Top each sandwich with an egg.
cheese béchamel Melt butter in small saucepan, add flour; cook, stirring, until mixture bubbles and thickens. Gradually add milk; cook, stirring, until sauce boils and thickens. Remove from heat; stir in cheese and parsley.
nutritional count per serving 29.2g total fat (15.2g saturated fat); 2328kJ (557 cal); 38.6g carbohydrate; 32.3g protein; 5.8g fibre

croque madame

[preparation time 15 minutes cooking time 20 minutes serves 4]

Synonymous with French cuisine, croque madame, and her brother, croque monsieur (minus the egg), are that nation's answer to a toasted sandwich. Found on café menus from Paris to Toulouse, you can easily create this taste of France in your kitchen.

[**preparation time** 15 minutes **cooking time** 20 minutes **serves** 4]

asian-style fried egg with mushrooms

¼ cup (60ml) oyster sauce
1 tablespoon light soy sauce
2 teaspoons brown sugar
1 tablespoon peanut oil
1 small red onion (100g), sliced thinly
2 cloves garlic, sliced thinly
200g swiss brown mushrooms, sliced thickly
150g oyster mushrooms, sliced thickly
100g shiitake mushrooms, sliced thickly
peanut oil, for deep-frying
4 eggs

For an omelette with a difference, add the mushroom mixture from this recipe; when the egg is nearly set, top half the omelette with the mushrooms, then fold over to enclose the mixture.

1 Combine sauces and sugar in small bowl.
2 Heat oil in wok; stir-fry onion and garlic until onion softens. Add mushrooms; stir-fry 5 minutes. Add half the sauce mixture; stir-fry 5 minutes. Remove mushrooms from wok.
3 Meanwhile, heat oil for deep-frying over high heat in medium saucepan. Add one egg; fry 30 seconds. Turn egg with slotted spoon; fry 30 seconds. Drain egg on absorbent paper. Repeat with remaining eggs.
4 Serve mushrooms topped with egg; drizzle with remaining sauce mixture.
nutritional count per serving 14.5g total fat (3.2g saturated fat); 903kJ (216 cal); 7.9g carbohydrate; 11.7g protein; 4.6g fibre

pulses and grains

As a dried or canned food, pulses and grains are an excellent pantry staple. Combine with just a few other ingredients and you'll have a filling, satisfying and very nutritious meal. Legumes are high in both dietary and soluble fibre, meaning healthy bowels and lower cholesterol; they have a low GI rating and are packed with protein. As a result, pulses can be used as a suitable substitute for meat a couple of times a week; one less stop at the shops.

red curry lentils

[**preparation time** 5 minutes **cooking time** 15 minutes **serves** 4]

Serve with steamed rice and fresh coriander leaves, if you like. Chicken stock can be used in place of the vegetable stock in this recipe.

1 tablespoon olive oil
1 medium brown onion (150g), quartered
2 tablespoons red curry paste
2 x 400g cans brown lentils, rinsed, drained
1 cup (250ml) vegetable stock
200g green beans, halved
2 tablespoons lime juice
⅔ cup (190g) yogurt

1   Heat oil in medium saucepan; cook onion, stirring, until soft. Add paste; cook, stirring, until fragrant. Add lentils and stock; bring to the boil. Reduce heat; simmer, uncovered, about 10 minutes or until stock has thickened. Add beans, simmer 2 minutes. Remove from heat; stir in juice.
2   Divide curry among serving bowls; serve topped with yogurt.
nutritional count per serving **10.5g total fat (2.2g saturated fat); 865kJ (207 cal); 14.3g carbohydrate; 11g protein; 6g fibre**

[**preparation time** 10 minutes **cooking time** 25 minutes **serves** 4]

chilli con carne with quesadillas

1 tablespoon olive oil

300g beef mince

1 medium red onion (170g), chopped finely

2 cloves garlic, crushed

1 tablespoon worcestershire sauce

1 tablespoon Tabasco sauce

2 teaspoons ground cumin

2 teaspoons ground coriander

1 teaspoon dried oregano

400g can crushed tomatoes

½ cup (130g) chunky tomato salsa

400g can kidney beans, rinsed, drained

400g can chickpeas, rinsed, drained

quesadillas

¾ cup (90g) coarsely grated cheddar cheese

4 x 20cm flour tortillas

20g butter

1 Heat half the oil in medium saucepan; cook beef, stirring, until browned, remove from pan. Heat remaining oil in same pan; cook onion and garlic, stirring, until onion softens. Return beef to pan with sauces, cumin, coriander and oregano; cook, stirring, 2 minutes.

2 Add undrained tomatoes then stir in salsa, beans and chickpeas; cook, uncovered, 10 minutes.

3 Meanwhile, make quesadillas. Serve chilli with quesadillas.

quesadillas Divide the cheese between two tortillas; top with remaining tortillas, pressing firmly to seal. Heat butter in medium frying pan; cook until browned both sides. Cut each quesadilla into quarters.

nutritional count per serving 26.8g total fat (11.1g saturated fat); 2562kJ (613 cal); 51.7g carbohydrate; 35.5g protein; 11.6g fibre

If you have some, add ⅓ cup loosely packed fresh coriander leaves to the chilli con carne just before serving.

600g piece jap pumpkin, chopped coarsely
1 tablespoon olive oil
1 medium red onion (170g), sliced thinly
2 cloves garlic, sliced thinly
2 tablespoons tomato paste
2 tablespoons red wine vinegar
400g can crushed tomatoes
½ cup (125ml) water
1 teaspoon ground allspice
400g can chickpeas, rinsed, drained

1   Preheat oven to 220°C/200°C fan-forced.
2   Place pumpkin, in single layer, on oven tray;
drizzle with half the oil. Roast, uncovered, about
20 minutes or until tender.
3   Heat remaining oil in large saucepan; cook
onion and garlic, stirring, until onion softens. Add
paste; cook, stirring, 1 minute. Add vinegar; cook,
stirring, 1 minute. Add undrained tomatoes, the
water, allspice, chickpeas and pumpkin; bring
to the boil. Simmer 5 minutes.

nutritional count per serving 6.8g total fat
(1.3g saturated fat); 899kJ (215 cal);
25.3g carbohydrate; 9.1g protein; 7.4g fibre

pumpkin and chickpea ratatouille

[preparation time 15 minutes cooking time 20 minutes serves 4]

Stir ⅓ cup of loosely
packed fresh basil
leaves into steamed
couscous for a tasty
accompaniment to
the ratatouille.

Typical Southern food in the USA, red beans and rice is a filling and budget-friendly dish. If you like, serve with grilled chicken for a meatier meal.

[**preparation time** 20 minutes **cooking time** 40 minutes **serves** 4]

red beans and rice

2 rindless bacon rashers (130g), chopped coarsely
1 medium brown onion (150g), chopped finely
1 small red capsicum (150g), chopped finely
2 cloves garlic, crushed
1 tablespoon tomato paste
1 tablespoon red wine vinegar
1 teaspoon smoked paprika
2 cups (400g) white long-grain rice
1 bay leaf
1 cup (250ml) chicken stock
2¼ cups (560ml) water
400g can kidney beans, rinsed, drained
½ cup (80g) frozen corn kernels
1 tablespoon lime juice

1   Cook bacon in a heated large frying pan, stirring, until starting to crisp. Add onion, capsicum and garlic; cook, stirring until capsicum softens.
2   Add paste, vinegar and paprika; cook, stirring, 1 minute. Add rice; cook, stirring, 2 minutes.
3   Add bay leaf, stock, the water and beans, bring to the boil; reduce heat, simmer, covered, 20 minutes. Add corn; cook, covered, about 5 minutes or until rice is tender. Remove from heat; stand, covered, 5 minutes. Stir in juice.
nutritional count per serving **3.3g total fat** (1g saturated fat); 2215kJ (530 cal); 99.3g carbohydrate; 20.8g protein; 7.1g fibre

[**preparation time** 15 minutes **cooking time** 1 hour **serves** 4]

oven-baked tuna risotto

3½ cups (875ml) chicken stock
10g butter
2 teaspoons olive oil
1 medium brown onion (150g), chopped finely
1 clove garlic, crushed
1½ cups (300g) arborio rice
425g can tuna in oil, drained
1 cup (120g) frozen peas
250g cherry tomatoes, halved
2 tablespoons lemon juice

Oven-baked is the perfect way to make risotto if you're pressed for time – it requires far less attention than the traditional-style risotto, but with equally delicious results.
Just before serving, stir in ⅓ cup loosely packed fresh basil leaves, if you like.

1   Preheat oven to 180°C/160°C fan-forced.
2   Bring stock to the boil in medium saucepan.
3   Meanwhile, melt butter with oil in large saucepan; cook onion and garlic, stirring, until onion softens. Add rice; stir to coat in onion mixture. Stir in hot stock and tuna.
4   Place risotto mixture in a large 2.5 litre (10-cup) shallow baking dish; cover with foil. Bake, in oven, 15 minutes, stirring halfway through cooking time. Uncover; bake 20 minutes. Stir in peas, top with tomato; bake, uncovered, about 15 minutes or until rice is tender. Remove from oven, stir in juice.

nutritional count per serving 25.8g total fat (5.2g saturated fat); 2583kJ (618 cal); 66.3g carbohydrate; 28g protein; 4g fibre

You need 12 bamboo skewers for this recipe; to prevent skewers from scorching, soak in cold water for at least 20 minutes before using.

[**preparation time** 20 minutes **cooking time** 35 minutes **serves** 4]

lamb kofta and brown rice salad

1 cup (200g) brown long-grain rice
½ cup (75g) seeded black olives, halved
1 small red capsicum (150g), chopped coarsely
1 tablespoon olive oil
¼ cup (60ml) lemon juice
¼ cup coarsely chopped fresh flat-leaf parsley
⅔ cup (130g) fetta cheese
500g lamb mince
1 cup (70g) stale breadcrumbs
1 small brown onion (80g), chopped finely
1 clove garlic, crushed
1 tablespoon garam masala
2 tablespoons yogurt

1 Cook rice in large saucepan of boiling water, uncovered, until tender; drain. Rinse under cold water; drain well.
2 Combine rice in large bowl with olives, capsicum, oil, 2 tablespoons of the juice and half the parsley; top with crumbled cheese.
3 Meanwhile, combine remaining ingredients with remaining juice and parsley in medium bowl; roll mixture into 12 balls, then roll balls into sausage shapes. Thread skewers through centre of kofta. Cook on heated oiled grill plate (or grill or barbecue), until cooked through.
nutritional count per serving **26g total fat (11.8g saturated fat); 2642kJ (632 cal); 59.2g carbohydrate; 38.7g protein; 2.4g fibre**

2 x 150g smoked ocean trout portions,
   skinned, flaked
400g can chickpeas, rinsed, drained
½ lebanese cucumber (65g), chopped finely
1 tablespoon lemon juice
3 teaspoons sumac
vegetable oil, for shallow-frying
4 x 20cm flour tortillas
yogurt dip
⅔ cup (190g) yogurt
½ lebanese cucumber (65g), chopped finely
1 teaspoon sumac

1 Combine fish, chickpeas, cucumber, juice and
sumac in medium bowl.
2 Heat oil in small frying pan; fry tortillas, one at
a time, until browned lightly both sides. Drain on
absorbent paper.
3 Meanwhile, make yogurt dip.
4 Serve tortillas topped with trout mixture; dollop
with yogurt dip.
yogurt dip Combine ingredients in small bowl.
nutritional count per serving 11.2g total fat
(2.2g saturated fat); 1442kJ (345 cal);
37.6g carbohydrate; 20.7g protein; 4.9g fibre

moroccan-flavoured smoked trout and chickpeas

[preparation time 15 minutes cooking time 5 minutes serves 4]

If you prefer, you can use regular cooked ocean
trout, rather than smoked, in this recipe.
Serve with mixed salad greens if you have some.
Add an extra dimension to the yogurt by stirring
in ¼ cup finely chopped fresh mint.

[**preparation time** 20 minutes **cooking time** 45 minutes **serves** 4]

pumpkin and chorizo risotto

1.5 litres (6 cups) chicken stock
500g butternut pumpkin, cut into 2cm pieces
1 tablespoon olive oil
2 smoked chorizo (340g), halved lengthways
10g butter
1 small brown onion (80g), chopped finely
1 clove garlic, crushed
1½ cups (300g) arborio rice
1 teaspoon ground cumin
½ cup (40g) finely grated parmesan cheese
½ cup coarsely chopped fresh flat-leaf parsley

Leftover risotto
makes great risotto
cakes; simply shape
cold risotto into
patties, then pan-fry
until browned lightly
on both sides.
Serve this risotto
with a rocket and
parmesan salad, if
you like.

1   Preheat oven to 220°C/200°C fan-forced.
2   Bring stock to the boil in medium saucepan. Reduce heat; simmer, covered.
3   Combine pumpkin with oil on oven tray. Roast, uncovered, about
25 minutes or until tender.
4   Meanwhile, cook chorizo in heated medium saucepan until browned;
slice thinly.
5   Melt butter in same pan; cook onion and garlic, stirring, until onion softens.
Add rice and cumin; stir to coat in onion mixture.
6   Stir in 1 cup of simmering stock; cook, stirring, over low heat until liquid
is absorbed. Continue adding stock in 1 cup batches, stirring, until absorbed
after each addition. Total cooking time should be about 35 minutes or until
rice is tender. Stir in pumpkin, chorizo, cheese and parsley; serve immediately.
nutritional count per serving 38.5g total fat (14.8g saturated fat); 3248kJ
(777 cal); 73.4g carbohydrate; 33g protein; 3.2g fibre

1½ cups (300g) yellow split peas
2 rindless bacon rashers (130g),
    chopped coarsely
6 thin sausages (480g), chopped coarsely
1 medium carrot (120g), chopped coarsely
1 trimmed celery stalk (100g), chopped coarsely
1 medium brown onion (150g), chopped coarsely
2 cloves garlic, sliced thinly
250g grape tomatoes, halved
400g can white beans, rinsed, drained
2 teaspoons finely grated orange rind
⅓ cup (80ml) orange juice

1 Place peas in medium bowl, cover with
cold water; stand overnight. Drain peas, rinse
under cold water; drain.
2 Place peas in medium saucepan, cover
with boiling water. Simmer, covered, about
10 minutes or until peas are tender; rinse
under cold water, drain.
3 Meanwhile, cook bacon and sausage in large
heated saucepan, in batches, until sausage
is cooked.
4 Add carrot, celery, onion and garlic to pan;
cook, stirring, until carrot softens slightly. Add
tomatoes; cook, stirring, 2 minutes. Add beans,
peas, bacon and sausage; stir to combine.
Remove from heat; stir in rind and juice.
nutritional count per serving 33.9g total fat
(15.1g saturated fat); 2985kJ (714 cal);
51.2g carbohydrate; 43g protein; 16.8g fibre

warm split pea and sausage salad

[**preparation time** 15 minutes (plus standing time) **cooking time** 25 minutes **serves** 4]

If you have some, stir
⅓ cup loosely packed
coarsely chopped fresh
flat-leaf parsley into
this recipe.
We used thin lamb
merguez sausages.

A loaf of fresh, crusty white bread, such as ciabatta, goes well with this soup. Prepared basil pesto is available from supermarkets and delicatessens. If you like, rocket pesto can be substituted for the basil pesto.

[**preparation time** 10 minutes **cooking time** 25 minutes **serves** 4]

soup au pistou

1 tablespoon olive oil
1 small brown onion (80g), chopped finely
2 cloves garlic, sliced thinly
1 large carrot (180g), chopped finely
1 trimmed celery stalk (100g), chopped finely
1 medium potato (200g), cut into 1cm cubes
⅓ cup (75g) risoni
3 cups (750ml) chicken stock
1 cup (250ml) water
400g can white beans, rinsed, drained
2 tablespoons lemon juice
⅓ cup (90g) basil pesto

1 Heat oil in large saucepan, add onion, garlic, carrot and celery; cook, stirring, until onion softens. Add potato, risoni, stock and the water; bring to the boil. Reduce heat; cook about 10 minutes or until risoni is tender.
2 Stir in beans; cook, uncovered, 1 minute.
3 Remove from heat; stir in juice. Serve with basil pesto.
nutritional count per serving **14.8g total fat (3g saturated fat); 1342kJ (321 cal); 31.4g carbohydrate; 12g protein; 7.5g fibre**

[**preparation time** 15 minutes **cooking time** 10 minutes **serves** 4]

felafel

It's important that you measure the bicarbonate of soda exactly, otherwise you will find that the felafel is tainted with the taste of excess soda. It's a good idea to sift the soda as it's often lumpy.
Popular served as part of a mezze, as a filling in pitta bread or enjoyed with salad, this Middle-Eastern snack is sure to be a hit with the whole family. If you're entertaining guests, felafel makes a great cocktail snack. Hummus also tastes great with felafel.

2 x 400g cans chickpeas, rinsed, drained
1 clove garlic, chopped coarsely
1 small brown onion (80g), chopped coarsely
1 tablespoon olive oil
1 egg
2 teaspoons ground cumin
½ teaspoon bicarbonate of soda
2 tablespoons plain flour
vegetable oil, for shallow-frying
4 large pitta breads (320g), warmed
yogurt sauce
1 cup (280g) yogurt
½ clove garlic, crushed
1 tablespoon lemon juice
½ teaspoon cayenne pepper

1   Process chickpeas, garlic, onion and olive oil until ingredients begin to combine; transfer mixture to medium bowl. Stir in egg, cumin, soda and flour until combined. Shape mixture into 12 patties.
2   Heat vegetable oil in large frying pan; cook felafel, in batches, until browned. Drain on absorbent paper.
3   Meanwhile, make yogurt sauce.
4   Serve felafel on pitta, topped with yogurt sauce. You can serve the felafel with a rocket and tomato salad.
yogurt sauce   Combine ingredients in small bowl.
nutritional count per serving   21.8g total fat (4.3g saturated fat); 2416kJ (575 cal); 68.3g carbohydrate; 21.7g protein; 9.1g fibre

[preparation time 15 minutes cooking time 20 minutes serves 4]

cranberry and pine nut pilaf with chicken

30g butter
1 tablespoon olive oil
1 medium brown onion (150g), chopped finely
1 trimmed celery stalk (100g), chopped finely
1½ cups (300g) basmati rice, rinsed, drained
1 bay leaf
1 cinnamon stick
1 litre (4 cups) chicken stock
²⁄₃ cup (160ml) water
400g chicken breast fillets
1 cup (250ml) dry white wine
¹⁄₃ cup (45g) dried cranberries
30g butter, extra
¹⁄₃ cup (50g) roasted pine nuts
1 tablespoon lemon juice

Currants can be used in place of the dried cranberries. If you have some, stir in ¹⁄₃ cup loosely packed coarsely chopped fresh flat-leaf parsley to the pilaf just before serving.

1 Melt butter with half the oil in medium saucepan; cook onion and celery, stirring, until celery softens. Add rice, bay leaf and cinnamon stick; cook, stirring, 2 minutes. Add stock and the water; bring to the boil. Reduce heat; simmer, covered, about 15 minutes or until rice is tender and liquid is absorbed.
2 Meanwhile, heat remaining oil in a large frying pan. Cook chicken until browned and cooked through. Remove from heat. Cover to keep warm.
3 Pour wine into same pan; bring to the boil. Reduce heat; simmer, uncovered, until liquid is reduced by half. Stir in cranberries and extra butter; add to rice mixture, stir until combined.
4 Fluff pilaf with fork; stir in nuts and juice. Serve with sliced chicken.
nutritional count per serving 29.5g total fat (10.5g saturated fat); 3068kJ (734 cal); 72.2g carbohydrate; 33.2g protein; 2.7g fibre

There's nothing better than an easy-to-make, easy-to-eat dinner, and this recipe is just that. Serve the soup with toasted turkish bread.

[**preparation time** 15 minutes **cooking time** 30 minutes **serves** 4]

white bean and chickpea soup with risoni

1 tablespoon olive oil
1 medium brown onion (150g), chopped coarsely
1 large carrot (180g), chopped coarsely
2 cloves garlic, sliced thinly
2 tablespoons tomato paste
2 teaspoons ground cumin
2 x 400g cans crushed tomatoes
1 litre (4 cups) vegetable stock
400g can chickpeas, rinsed, drained
400g can white beans, rinsed, drained
⅓ cup (75g) risoni

1 Heat oil in large saucepan; cook onion and carrot, stirring, until carrot softens. Add garlic, paste and cumin; cook, stirring, until garlic softens.
2 Add undrained tomatoes and stock to pan; bring to the boil. Add chickpeas and beans; return to the boil. Add risoni; boil about 10 minutes or until risoni is tender.

nutritional count per serving **7.8g total fat (1.4g saturated fat); 1359kJ (325 cal); 41.9g carbohydrate; 15.5g protein; 11.6g fibre**

500g frozen broad beans
400g can white beans, rinsed, drained
½ small red onion (50g), sliced thinly
1 lebanese cucumber (130g), chopped coarsely
1 teaspoon finely grated lemon rind
2 tablespoons lemon juice
1 tablespoon olive oil
300g smoked salmon
fried capers
¼ cup (50g) capers, rinsed, drained
¼ cup (60ml) olive oil

1   Boil, steam or microwave broad beans until just tender. Peel; place in medium bowl. Add white beans, onion, cucumber, rind, juice and oil; toss to combine.
2   Meanwhile, make fried capers.
3   Top salmon slices with fried capers; serve with salad, and lemon wedges, if you like.
fried capers Pat capers dry with absorbent paper. Heat oil in shallow small frying pan; add capers carefully (they will splatter). Fry for about 2 minutes; drain on absorbent paper.
nutritional count per serving **22.2g total fat (3.2g saturated fat); 1705kJ (408 cal); 18.7g carbohydrate; 27.3g protein; 13.2g fibre**

white and broad bean salad with smoked salmon

[**preparation time** 20 minutes **cooking time** 5 minutes **serves** 4]

This recipe is perfect for 8 people when served as a starter. Fried capers are also delicious in salads and sprinkled over side dishes such as grilled asparagus.

the mighty potato

The mighty potato is a staple around the world for good reason. They're inexpensive, filling, delicious and nutritious. And there are myriad ways you can cook them; quick and easy, or slow and meltingly delicious. Potatoes last for up to three weeks in a cool, dry place such as your cupboard, so having them as a pantry staple makes for an easy last-minute meal.

potato and pea curry

[**preparation time** 15 minutes **cooking time** 25 minutes **serves** 4]

3 medium potatoes (600g), chopped coarsely
1 tablespoon vegetable oil
2 cloves garlic, crushed
2cm piece fresh ginger (10g), grated
¼ cup (75g) tikka masala curry paste
300ml cream
1½ cups (180g) frozen peas
½ cup (140g) yogurt
2 tablespoons lime juice
4 small pappadams
4 hard-boiled eggs, halved

We used tikka masala in this recipe – this medium-mild curry paste is made from a colourful combination of chilli, coriander, cumin, lentil flour, garlic, ginger, oil, turmeric, fennel, pepper, cloves, cinnamon and cardamom; however, you can use whatever curry paste takes your fancy. The traditional way to cook pappadams is to deep-fry them, but the microwave oven method works well, too.

1   Boil, steam or microwave potato until just tender; drain.
2   Meanwhile, heat oil in large saucepan; cook garlic and ginger, stirring, 2 minutes. Add paste; cook, stirring, until fragrant.
3   Add cream, bring to the boil; reduce heat. Add potato; simmer, uncovered, 5 minutes. Add peas and yogurt; stir over low heat about 5 minutes or until peas are heated through. Stir in juice.
4   Cook pappadams, in microwave oven, following packet instructions.
5   Top curry with egg; serve with pappadams.
nutritional count per serving 51.8g total fat (25.5g saturated fat); 3106kJ (743 cal); 37.8g carbohydrate; 22.7g protein; 24.5g fibre

[**preparation time** 20 minutes **cooking time** 25 minutes **serves** 4]

kumara and orange salad

Segment the oranges over a small bowl, reserving 1 tablespoon of the juice to use in the orange dressing. You can add ⅓ cup loosely packed fresh flat-leaf parsley to the salad if you have some.

2 medium kumara (800g), cut into wedges
2 tablespoons olive oil
1 teaspoon ground cumin
½ teaspoon ground nutmeg
½ cup (100g) couscous
½ cup (125ml) boiling water
2 medium oranges (480g), segmented
½ cup (65g) dried cranberries
⅓ cup (40g) pecans, roasted
orange balsamic dressing
1 tablespoon orange juice
1 tablespoon balsamic vinegar
1 teaspoon dijon mustard
1 clove garlic, crushed
2 tablespoons olive oil

1 Preheat oven to 220°C/200°C fan-forced.
2 Combine kumara, oil, cumin and nutmeg on oven tray; roast, uncovered, about 25 minutes or until kumara is tender.
3 Meanwhile, combine couscous with the water in large heatproof bowl; cover, stand about 5 minutes or until water is absorbed.
4 Make orange balsamic dressing.
5 Combine orange, cranberries and pecans with couscous. Serve kumara with couscous and dressing.
orange balsamic dressing Place ingredients in screw-top jar; shake well.
nutritional count per serving **21.3g total fat (2.4g saturated fat); 1856kJ (444 cal); 51.5g carbohydrate; 8.4g protein; 6.3g fibre**

5 medium potatoes (1kg), sliced thinly
1 large brown onion (200g), sliced thinly
9 anchovy fillets, drained, halved lengthways
¼ cup (60ml) lemon juice
¾ cup (180ml) cream
2 tablespoons stale breadcrumbs
2 tablespoons finely chopped
    fresh flat-leaf parsley
30g butter

1 Preheat oven to 220°C/200°C fan-forced. Grease medium-deep 22cm-square baking dish.
2 Layer a third of the potato over base of dish; sprinkle over a third of the onion and a third of the anchovy. Sprinkle with 1 tablespoon of the juice. Repeat with remaining potato, onion, anchovy and juice. Pour over cream; sprinkle breadcrumbs and parsley over top then dot with butter.
3 Bake, covered, about 1 hour or until potato is tender. Uncover; bake about 15 minutes or until browned lightly.
nutritional count per serving **26.5g total fat (17.1g saturated fat); 1868kJ (447 cal); 39.2g carbohydrate; 10.5g protein; 6g fibre**

janssen's temptation

This is our take on the traditional Swedish recipe of the same name. Even if you're not a lover of anchovies, we're certain you'll love this dish.
Try serving this dish with a green salad, dressed with a lemon vinaigrette.

[**preparation time** 15 minutes **cooking time** 1 hour 15 minutes **serves** 4]

This is our twist on a caesar salad – the addition of potato makes this recipe suitable for a quick dinner or an easy option for lunch at work. For a low-fat version, replace the mayonnaise with skim-milk natural yogurt.
The breadcrumbs can be toasted in the oven instead of frying them.

[**preparation time** 15 minutes **cooking time** 10 minutes **serves** 4]

caesar-style potato salad

2kg potatoes, chopped coarsely
25g butter
½ cup (35g) stale bread slices, cut into
    1cm pieces
2 trimmed celery stalks (200g), sliced thinly
1 cup (180g) cornichons, halved lengthways
caesar dressing
⅔ cup (190g) mayonnaise
2 tablespoons dijon mustard
1 clove garlic, crushed
2 tablespoons lemon juice
1 tablespoon worcestershire sauce
1 tablespoon milk

1 Boil, steam or microwave potato until tender; drain.
2 Meanwhile, make dressing.
3 Melt butter in small frying pan; cook bread cubes over low heat, stirring, until browned lightly.
4 Combine potato, celery, cornichons and dressing in large bowl; sprinkle with croutons.
caesar dressing Whisk ingredients in small bowl until combined.
nutritional count per serving **21.5g total fat (5.4g saturated fat); 2508kJ (600 cal); 80.9g carbohydrate; 14.3g protein; 12.2g fibre**

[**preparation time** 20 minutes **cooking time** 1 hour 10 minutes **serves** 4]

baked potatoes with salmon and peas

4 large potatoes (1.2kg), unpeeled
½ cup (60g) frozen peas
50g butter, softened
½ cup (120g) sour cream
100g smoked salmon, chopped coarsely
2 tablespoons coarsely chopped fresh dill

If you don't like dill, stir a teaspoon of ground paprika through the potato mixture instead. Hot, sweet and smoky paprika all have quite different tastes, any of them will be fine for this recipe.

1 Preheat oven to 180°C/160°C fan-forced.
2 Pierce skin of potatoes with fork; wrap each potato in foil, place on oven tray. Bake about 1 hour or until tender.
3 Meanwhile, boil, steam or microwave peas until tender; drain.
4 Combine butter and sour cream in medium bowl.
5 Remove potatoes from oven; fold back foil to reveal tops of potatoes. Increase temperature to 240°C/220°C fan-forced.
6 Cut 0.5cm from top of each potato; chop coarsely, add to bowl with butter mixture. Carefully scoop out flesh from potatoes, leaving skins intact. Add potato flesh to butter mixture.
7 Mash potato mixture until almost smooth; stir in peas, salmon and dill. Divide among potato shells.
8 Bake about 10 minutes or until browned lightly.
nutritional count per serving 22.7g total fat (14.8g saturated fat); 1873kJ (448 cal); 41.1g carbohydrate; 14.6g protein; 6.9g fibre

Perfect for breakfast, lunch or dinner, this recipe can easily be doubled to feed a starving army of kids. Poached or fried eggs complement this recipe well, as does a side serving of toast.

[**preparation time** 10 minutes **cooking time** 25 minutes **serves** 4]

bacon and potato hash

8 rindless bacon rashers (500g)
3 medium potatoes (600g), cut into 1cm pieces
1 large red capsicum (350g), chopped coarsely
5g butter
3 shallots (75g), chopped coarsely
½ teaspoon smoked paprika
lemon vinaigrette
1 teaspoon dijon mustard
2 tablespoons lemon juice
1 tablespoon olive oil

1 Cook bacon in heated large frying pan, in batches, until beginning to crisp. Coarsely chop half the bacon; keep warm.
2 Meanwhile, boil, steam or microwave potato and capsicum, separately, until almost tender; drain well.
3 Make lemon vinaigrette.
4 Melt butter in same frying pan; add potato, cook, stirring occasionally, about 10 minutes or until browned lightly. Add shallot, paprika, chopped bacon and capsicum; cook, stirring, until shallot softens. Remove from heat; drizzle with vinaigrette.
5 Serve hash topped with remaining bacon.
lemon vinaigrette Place ingredients in screw-top jar; shake well.
nutritional count per serving **12.8g total fat (3.8g saturated fat); 1454kJ (348 cal); 24.1g carbohydrate; 31.8g protein; 4g fibre**

10 small potatoes (1.2kg), sliced thickly
¼ cup (60ml) olive oil
2 tablespoons wholegrain mustard
1 tablespoon white wine vinegar
2 tablespoons lemon juice
½ small red onion (50g), sliced thinly
425g tuna in springwater, drained, flaked
500g frozen broad beans

1 Boil, steam or microwave potato until tender; drain.
2 Whisk oil, mustard, vinegar and juice in small bowl.
3 Combine potato in large bowl with dressing, onion and tuna.
4 Meanwhile, boil, steam or microwave beans until just tender. Peel; add to potato salad. Toss gently to serve.

nutritional count per serving 16.7g total fat (2.8g saturated fat); 2190kJ (524 cal); 49.9g carbohydrate; 35.2g protein; 15.7g fibre

warm potato and broad bean salad with tuna

[preparation time 20 minutes cooking time 10 minutes serves 4]

A grilled tuna steak would also taste terrific in place of the canned tuna in this salad.
Peas or snow peas can be used instead of the broad beans.

47

[**preparation time** 25 minutes (plus refrigeration time) **cooking time** 1 hour **serves** 4]

thai potato and salmon rösti

4 medium potatoes (800g)
1 teaspoon coarse cooking salt
1 tablespoon fish sauce
1 tablespoon red curry paste
1 tablespoon lime juice
1 tablespoon plain flour
415g can pink salmon, drained
1 tablespoon coarsely chopped fresh coriander
vegetable oil, for shallow-frying
cucumber dipping sauce
1 lebanese cucumber (130g), seeded, sliced thinly
½ cup (125ml) water
¼ cup (55g) white sugar
¼ cup (60ml) white wine vinegar
1 teaspoon sambal oelek

You can skip the coriander in this recipe, if you like; it will still taste great.
This recipe makes an excellent party snack; just shape the patties into bite-sized pieces, and serve on a platter with the dipping sauce.

1 Grate potatoes coarsely into large bowl; stir in salt, squeeze out excess moisture. Stir in sauce, paste, juice, flour, salmon and coriander. Shape mixture into twelve 8cm-wide patties. Place on tray, cover; refrigerate 30 minutes.
2 Meanwhile, make cucumber dipping sauce.
3 Heat oil in large frying pan; cook rösti, in batches, until browned and heated through. Serve rösti with sauce.
cucumber dipping sauce Place cucumber in heatproof bowl. Combine the water, sugar and vinegar in small saucepan; stir over heat, without boiling, until sugar is dissolved. Remove from heat; stir in sambal. Pour over cucumber.
nutritional count per serving **32.4g total fat (4.9g saturated fat); 2395kJ (573 cal); 43.6g carbohydrate; 24.5g protein; 5.2g fibre**

5 medium potatoes (1kg), halved
¼ cup (60ml) olive oil
2 tablespoons balsamic vinegar
½ small red onion (50g), chopped finely
¼ cup (50g) rinsed, drained baby capers
850g can baby beetroot, drained, quartered
3 hard-boiled eggs, quartered

1   Preheat oven to 220°C/200°C fan-forced.
2   Cook potato in large saucepan of boiling water
5 minutes; drain. Cut potato into wedges, combine
with 1 tablespoon of the oil on oven tray. Roast,
uncovered, about 45 minutes or until potato is
browned lightly.
3   Meanwhile, whisk vinegar and remaining oil
in small bowl.
4   Place potato in large bowl with onion, capers
and beetroot; drizzle with dressing. Top salad
with egg; serve warm.
nutritional count per serving 18g total fat
(3.1g saturated fat); 1777kJ (425 cal);
48g carbohydrate; 13.2g protein; 9.1g fibre

warm potato and beetroot salad

For nicely crisped
potatoes, heat the
oven tray before
adding the potatoes.
You can sprinkle ¼ cup
chopped fresh chives
over the salad just
before serving.

[preparation time 10 minutes cooking time 45 minutes serves 4]

[**preparation time** 15 minutes **cooking time** 25 minutes **serves** 4]

You could also make this recipe
in a 1-litre (4-cup) baking dish.

potato and tuna bake

3 medium potatoes (600g), cut into 1cm pieces
20g butter
1 tablespoon olive oil
3 shallots (75g), chopped coarsely
425g can tuna in oil, drained
250g frozen spinach, thawed, drained
½ cup (125ml) milk
1½ cups (180g) coarsely grated cheddar cheese
½ cup drained semi-dried tomatoes,
    chopped coarsely

1   Preheat oven to 220°C/200°C fan-forced.
Oil four 1-cup (250ml) shallow baking dishes.
2   Boil, steam or microwave potato until almost
tender; drain.
3   Heat butter and oil in large frying pan; add
potato, cook, stirring occasionally, about
10 minutes or until browned lightly. Add shallot;
cook, stirring, until shallot softens. Transfer
mixture to medium bowl; coarsely crush potato
mixture with fork.
4   Stir tuna, spinach, milk, ½ cup of the cheese
and tomatoes into potato mixture. Divide mixture
among dishes; sprinkle with remaining cheese.
Bake, uncovered, in oven, about 10 minutes or
until browned lightly.
nutritional count per serving **38.8g total fat
(15.9g saturated fat); 2696kJ (645 cal);
28.6g carbohydrate; 41.5g protein; 8.8g fibre**

pasta perfect

Pasta is an undeniable favourite for a comforting, filling meal that is quick to prepare. Choose a suitable pasta for your pasta sauce; chunky sauces stick well to short or tubular pasta shapes, but use strands of pasta with creamy or simple sauces. Of course, you can use any pasta you have in your pantry. Dried pasta lasts a long time in your cupboard, but don't overlook fresh pasta kept in the freezer, including filled pasta shapes such as ravioli.

penne bolognese

[**preparation time** 15 minutes **cooking time** 1 hour **serves** 6]

We've used penne pasta in this recipe, but feel free to use spaghetti, if you prefer. Stir in ⅓ cup loosely packed fresh basil leaves just before serving, if you like.

2 tablespoons olive oil
1 small brown onion (80g), chopped finely
1 medium carrot (120g), chopped finely
1 trimmed celery stalk (100g), chopped finely
2 cloves garlic, sliced thinly
500g beef mince
500g pork mince
½ cup (125ml) milk
½ cup (125ml) dry white wine
2 x 400g cans crushed tomatoes
1 cup (250ml) beef stock
500g penne

1   Heat oil in large saucepan, add onion, carrot, celery and garlic; cook, stirring, until celery softens. Add minces; cook, stirring, until browned. Add milk and wine; simmer, uncovered, until liquid is almost evaporated. Add undrained tomatoes; cook, stirring, 5 minutes. Add stock; bring to the boil. Reduce heat; simmer, covered, 30 minutes.
2   Meanwhile, cook pasta in large saucepan of boiling water until tender; drain. Serve sauce with pasta.
nutritional count per serving **19.8g total fat (6.2g saturated fat); 2700kJ (646 cal); 64.4g carbohydrate; 45.7g protein; 5.6g fibre**

[**preparation time** 15 minutes **cooking time** 20 minutes **serves** 4]

chickpea, preserved lemon and risoni salad

French-trimmed lamb cutlets marry beautifully with this salad; simply grill the lamb until cooked as desired, squeeze with lemon juice and serve alongside the salad.

250g frozen peas
1¼ cups (275g) risoni
1 tablespoon olive oil
2 cloves garlic, crushed
1 trimmed celery stalk (100g), chopped finely
400g can chickpeas, rinsed, drained
2 pieces preserved lemon (70g), trimmed, chopped finely
⅓ cup (55g) seeded black olives
115g goat cheese, crumbled
yogurt dressing
⅓ cup (95g) greek-style yogurt
1 tablespoon white wine vinegar

1 Boil, steam or microwave peas until tender.
2 Meanwhile, make yogurt dressing.
3 Cook risoni in medium saucepan of boiling water, uncovered, until tender; drain.
4 Meanwhile, heat the oil in large frying pan; cook garlic and celery, stirring, until celery softens slightly. Stir in chickpeas, lemon, olives, risoni and peas. Sprinkle cheese over salad; drizzle with dressing.
yogurt dressing Whisk ingredients in small bowl until combined.
nutritional count per serving **13.4g total fat (5.1g saturated fat); 2052kJ (491 cal); 66g carbohydrate; 21g protein; 10.4g fibre**

[**preparation time** 15 minutes **cooking time** 55 minutes **serves** 6]

baked penne with kumara and spinach

2 medium red onions (340g), cut into wedges
2 small kumara (600g), sliced thickly
2 tablespoons olive oil
375g penne pasta
250g frozen spinach, thawed, drained
1½ cups (360g) ricotta cheese
1 clove garlic, crushed
¼ cup (60ml) cream
2 x 400g cans crushed tomatoes
¼ cup (40g) pine nuts
½ cup (40g) finely grated parmesan cheese

1 Preheat oven to 220°C/200°C fan-forced.
2 Combine onion and kumara with oil in large baking dish; roast, uncovered, stirring once, about 40 minutes or until tender.
3 Meanwhile, cook pasta in large saucepan of boiling water until tender; drain.
4 Combine pasta in large bowl with spinach, ricotta, garlic, cream and tomatoes.
5 Spread kumara mixture over base of 3-litre (12-cup) baking dish. Top with pasta mixture; sprinkle with nuts and parmesan. Bake, covered, 10 minutes. Uncover; bake about 5 minutes or until browned lightly.

nutritional count per serving **25.3g total fat (9.8g saturated fat); 2450kJ (586 cal); 63.4g carbohydrate; 21.9g protein; 8.4g fibre**

375g spaghetti
2 tablespoons olive oil
3 cloves garlic, sliced thinly
¼ cup (50g) rinsed, drained baby capers
10 anchovy fillets, chopped finely
1 tablespoon finely grated lemon rind
1 tablespoon lemon juice

1 Cook pasta in large saucepan of boiling water until tender; drain.
2 Meanwhile, heat oil in medium frying pan; cook garlic, stirring, until fragrant. Add capers and anchovies; stir gently until hot. Pour garlic mixture over pasta; stir in rind and juice.

nutritional count per serving **11.1g total fat (1.7g saturated fat); 1781kJ (426 cal); 65.6g carbohydrate; 13.3g protein; 3.8g fibre**

pasta with capers and anchovies

[**preparation time** 10 minutes **cooking time** 10 minutes **serves** 4]

A teaspoon of dried chilli flakes cooked with the garlic makes a deliciously hot alternative.
If you have some, stir in ¼ cup coarsely chopped fresh flat-leaf parsley or a handful of baby rocket leaves before serving.

[**preparation time** 15 minutes **cooking time** 25 minutes **serves** 4]

mixed mushroom stroganoff

375g fettuccine pasta
1 tablespoon olive oil
20g butter
3 shallots (75g), sliced thinly
2 cloves garlic, sliced thinly
3 teaspoons smoked paprika
2 tablespoons dijon mustard
350g button mushrooms, sliced thinly
200g swiss brown mushrooms, sliced thinly
200g shiitake mushrooms, sliced thinly
¼ cup (60ml) dry white wine
¾ cup (180ml) vegetable stock
1 cup (240g) sour cream

If you have some lean beef in the freezer, substitute half the mushrooms for the sliced beef, browning the beef in oil and returning it to the pan just before serving. You can stir ¼ cup coarsely chopped fresh flat-leaf parsley into the stroganoff just before serving.

1 Cook pasta in large saucepan of boiling water until tender; drain. Rinse under cold water, drain.
2 Meanwhile, heat oil and half the butter in large saucepan, add shallots and garlic; cook, stirring, until shallot softens. Add paprika and mustard; cook, stirring, 1 minute. Stir in mushrooms and remaining butter. Cover; cook 10 minutes, stirring occasionally. Add wine and stock; cook, uncovered, about 5 minutes or until liquid is reduced slightly. Add sour cream; simmer gently, uncovered, 5 minutes. Serve over pasta.

nutritional count per serving 34.4g total fat (19.3g saturated fat); 2863kJ (685 cal); 68.7g carbohydrate; 18.8g protein; 8.3g fibre

375g angel hair pasta
2 cups (240g) frozen peas
2 tablespoons olive oil
2 cloves garlic, sliced thinly
2 teaspoons finely grated lemon rind
½ cup (125ml) lemon juice
¾ cup (180g) ricotta cheese, crumbled

1   Cook pasta in large saucepan of boiling water until tender; add peas during last minute of pasta cooking time. Drain, reserving ¼ cup cooking liquid. Rinse pasta and peas under cold water; drain.
2   Meanwhile, heat oil in small frying pan; cook garlic, stirring, until fragrant.
3   Combine pasta and peas in large bowl with reserved cooking liquid, garlic mixture, rind and juice; stir in cheese.

nutritional count per serving 15.6g total fat (4.7g saturated fat); 2123kJ (508 cal); 69g carbohydrate; 19g protein; 6.9g fibre

lemon, pea and ricotta pasta

[preparation time 5 minutes cooking time 10 minutes serves 4]

Fetta cheese can be used in place of the ricotta cheese.
If you have some, stir ⅓ cup loosely packed fresh mint leaves into this recipe.

Baby capers can be added to this recipe. Stir in ⅓ cup coarsely chopped fresh basil leaves just before serving, if you like.

[**preparation time** 5 minutes **cooking time** 10 minutes **serves** 4]

tuna and chilli pasta

375g angel hair pasta
425g can tuna in oil
4 cloves garlic, sliced thinly
1 teaspoon dried chilli flakes
⅓ cup (80ml) dry white wine
400g can chopped tomatoes
1 tablespoon lemon juice

1   Cook pasta in large saucepan of boiling water until tender; drain, reserving ¼ cup cooking liquid. Rinse pasta under cold water, drain.
2   Meanwhile, drain tuna, reserving 2 tablespoons of the oil. Heat oil in medium frying pan, add garlic; cook, stirring, until fragrant. Add chilli and wine; cook, uncovered, until wine is almost evaporated. Add undrained tomatoes, tuna and reserved cooking liquid; simmer until liquid has reduced slightly. Remove from heat; stir in juice. Combine pasta and sauce in large bowl.
nutritional count per serving **22.3g total fat (3.2g saturated fat); 2617kJ (626 cal); 67.5g carbohydrate; 32.5g protein; 4.8g fibre**

[**preparation time** 15 minutes **cooking time** 35 minutes **serves** 4]

coconut-poached chicken on thai vermicelli salad

600g chicken breast fillets
1 cup (250ml) light coconut cream
1½ cups (375ml) chicken stock
1 tablespoon brown sugar
1 clove garlic, crushed
2cm piece fresh ginger (10g), grated
1 tablespoon fish sauce
2 tablespoons lime juice
125g rice vermicelli
1 small carrot (70g), sliced thinly
¼ cup (50g) rinsed, drained sliced bamboo shoots
¼ cup loosely packed fresh coriander leaves, chopped finely
¼ cup loosely packed fresh mint leaves, chopped finely

1 Place chicken in medium saucepan with cream, stock, sugar, garlic and ginger; bring to the boil. Reduce heat; simmer, uncovered, about 10 minutes or until cooked. Cool chicken in poaching liquid 10 minutes. Remove chicken from pan. Return poaching liquid to the boil; reduce to 1 cup. Remove from heat; stir in sauce and juice.
2 Meanwhile, place vermicelli in large heatproof bowl, cover with boiling water; stand until just tender, drain. Rinse under cold water; drain. Using scissors, cut vermicelli into random lengths.
3 Tear chicken coarsely. Place vermicelli in medium bowl with chicken, carrot and bamboo shoots; stir in poaching liquid. Serve sprinkled with herbs.
nutritional count per serving **11.5g total fat (7.9g saturated fat); 1346kJ (322 cal); 16.1g carbohydrate; 37.6g protein; 1.5g fibre**

[**preparation time** 15 minutes **cooking time** 5 minutes **serves** 4]

asian smoked trout salad with sambal dressing

Sambal oelek is an Indonesian paste made from ground chillies and vinegar; it can be purchased from supermarkets and Asian food shops. If you have some, serve the salad sprinkled with fresh coriander leaves or fresh mint leaves, for a refreshing taste.

125g rice vermicelli
2 x 150g smoked ocean trout portions, skinned, flaked
1 small carrot (70g), cut into matchstick-sized pieces
1 lebanese cucumber (130g), cut into matchstick-sized pieces
sambal dressing
1 tablespoon sambal oelek
1 tablespoon brown sugar
1 tablespoon fish sauce
¼ cup (60ml) lime juice
2 teaspoons sesame oil

1 Place vermicelli in large heatproof bowl, cover with boiling water; stand until tender, drain. Rinse under cold water; drain. Using scissors, cut vermicelli into random lengths.
2 Meanwhile, make sambal dressing.
3 Combine vermicelli, fish, carrot, cucumber and dressing in large bowl.
sambal dressing Combine ingredients in small bowl.
nutritional count per serving 6.6g total fat (1.2g saturated fat); 1062kJ (254 cal); 25.9g carbohydrate; 21.6g protein; 1.5g fibre

pizzas and pastry

Everyone loves pizza, kids and adults alike. Experiment with healthy toppings, or let kids make their own. Pizza bases freeze well and can be topped with one of the great suggestions here, or with anything leftover in the fridge. For last-minute, elegant entertaining, frozen puff, shortcrust or fillo pastry can make a stunning tart or pie that is much easier than you think and has an effortless grown-up edge.

potato and bacon pizza

[**preparation time** 15 minutes **cooking time** 20 minutes **serves** 4]

2 x 335g pizza bases
2 tablespoons olive oil
4 rindless bacon rashers (260g), chopped coarsely
2 cloves garlic, sliced thinly
1 tablespoon coarsely chopped fresh rosemary
½ teaspoon dried chilli flakes
500g potatoes, sliced thinly
1 cup (80g) finely grated parmesan cheese

We used large (25cm diameter) packaged pizza bases for this recipe. It's important to slice the potatoes as thinly as possible.

1 Preheat oven to 220°C/200°C fan-forced. Place pizza bases on oven trays; bake about 10 minutes or until crisp.
2 Meanwhile, heat oil in large frying pan; cook bacon, garlic, rosemary and chilli, stirring, 5 minutes. Remove mixture from pan.
3 Add potato to same heated pan; cook, stirring frequently, about 10 minutes or until tender.
4 Sprinkle each pizza base with ⅓ cup of the cheese. Divide bacon mixture and potato between bases; top with remaining cheese. Bake about 5 minutes.
nutritional count per serving **25.7g total fat (7.6g saturated fat); 3486kJ (834 cal); 105.6g carbohydrate; 39.6g protein; 9g fibre**

[**preparation time** 20 minutes **cooking time** 25 minutes **serves** 4]

moroccan tart

1 sheet ready-rolled shortcrust pastry, thawed
1 tablespoon olive oil
300g lamb mince
1 teaspoon ground coriander
½ teaspoon ground cinnamon
400g can chickpeas, rinsed, drained
1 clove garlic, crushed
2 tablespoons lemon juice
1 piece preserved lemon (35g), trimmed, chopped finely
2 tablespoons roasted pine nuts
125g fetta cheese, crumbled

You can top this tart
with finely chopped
fresh flat-leaf parsley
or mint leaves and
serve with a salad of
baby spinach and
orange segments.

1   Preheat oven to 200°C/180°C fan-forced.
2   Roll pastry out to 28cm x 30cm rectangle; place on oiled oven tray.
Fold edges of pastry over to make a 1cm border all the way around pastry.
Prick pastry base with fork; bake 10 minutes.
3   Meanwhile, heat half the oil in medium frying pan; cook lamb, coriander
and cinnamon, stirring, 5 minutes. Drain away excess oil.
4   Combine chickpeas, garlic, juice and remaining oil in medium bowl.
Using fork, coarsely mash mixture; stir in preserved lemon. Spread over
pastry base. Top with lamb mixture; sprinkle with nuts and cheese. Bake,
in oven, about 10 minutes.
nutritional count per serving **34.8g total fat (14.3g saturated fat); 2274kJ
(544 cal); 27.7g carbohydrate; 28.4g protein; 4.4g fibre**

[**preparation time** 10 minutes **cooking time** 15 minutes **serves** 4]

We used large (25cm diameter) packaged pizza bases for this recipe.
You can scatter 2 tablespoons of fresh oregano leaves over the pizza just before serving.

artichoke, anchovy and chilli pizza

2 x 335g pizza bases
⅓ cup (95g) tomato paste
⅔ cup (80g) grated cheddar cheese
10 drained marinated artichokes (600g), quartered
10 anchovy fillets, drained
½ teaspoon dried chilli flakes
¼ cup (20g) finely grated parmesan cheese

1 Preheat oven to 220°C/200°C fan-forced. Place pizza bases on oven trays.
2 Spread bases with paste; divide cheddar cheese between bases. Top with artichoke and anchovies; sprinkle with chilli and parmesan cheese. Bake about 15 minutes.
nutritional count per serving **19g total fat (7.1g saturated fat); 2826kJ (676 cal); 93.8g carbohydrate; 28g protein; 7.2g fibre**

2 x 335g pizza bases
300g sour cream
1 tablespoon prepared horseradish
2 tablespoons coarsely chopped rinsed,
    drained capers
2 tablespoons lemon juice
400g smoked salmon
½ small red onion (50g), sliced thinly
2 tablespoons coarsely chopped fresh dill

1   Preheat oven to 220°C/200°C fan-forced.
2   Place pizza bases on oven trays. Bake about
10 minutes or until browned; cool.
3   Meanwhile, combine sour cream, horseradish,
capers and half the juice in medium bowl; spread
over bases.
4   Top with salmon and onion; sprinkle with
remaining juice and dill.
nutritional count per serving 41.4g total fat
(21.6g saturated fat); 3846kJ (920 cal);
93.3g carbohydrate; 40.2g protein; 6.6g fibre

smoked salmon pizza

[preparation time 10 minutes cooking time 10 minutes serves 4]

We used large (25cm diameter) packaged pizza
bases for this recipe.
Be sure to use prepared horseradish rather than
horseradish cream – the latter is a commercially
prepared creamy paste made from horseradish,
vinegar, oil and sugar. Prepared horseradish is
preserved grated horseradish root.

[**preparation time** 15 minutes (plus freezing time) **cooking time** 35 minutes **serves** 4]

caramelised onion tarts

40g butter
1 tablespoon olive oil
3 large brown onions (600g), sliced thinly
2 tablespoons brown sugar
2 tablespoons balsamic vinegar
½ cup (125ml) water
2 sheets ready-rolled puff pastry
¼ cup (60g) ricotta cheese

If you don't have four 12cm loose-based flan tins, you can make one large tart instead. These tarts are not baked with baking weights so the pastry will puff up. Gently push the pastry down when topping it with the onion, to create a rustic-looking tart.
This recipe goes well with a simple green salad.
If you have some, sprinkle 1 tablespoon of fresh thyme leaves over the tart just before serving.

1 Oil 4 x 12cm loose-based flan tins.
2 Melt butter with oil in large frying pan, add onion, sugar and vinegar; cook, stirring, until very soft and browned lightly. Add the water; cook, stirring, until water has evaporated.
3 Meanwhile, cut pastry sheets in half diagonally. Line tins with pastry, press into sides; trim edges, prick bases with fork. Freeze 15 minutes.
4 Preheat oven to 220°C/200°C fan-forced.
5 Place tins on oven tray; bake 15 minutes.
6 Top tarts with caramelised onion, gently push onion down to flatten pastry; sprinkle with cheese. Bake about 5 minutes.
nutritional count per serving **33.5g total fat (17.3g saturated fat); 2161kJ (517 cal); 44.6g carbohydrate; 8.4g protein; 3.1g fibre**

500g grape tomatoes
1 tablespoon balsamic vinegar
1 tablespoon olive oil
1 sheet ready-rolled puff pasty
2 tablespoons basil pesto
⅓ cup (55g) seeded black olives
1½ cups (360g) ricotta cheese

1   Preheat oven to 220°C/200°C fan-forced.
2   Combine tomatoes in medium bowl with
vinegar and half the oil; place on oven tray.
Roast, uncovered, about 10 minutes or until
tomatoes collapse.
3   Place pastry on oiled oven tray. Fold edges of
pastry over to make a 0.5cm border all the way
around pastry; prick base with fork. Place another
oven tray on top of pastry; bake 10 minutes.
Remove top tray from pastry; reduce temperature
to 200°C/180°C fan-forced.
4   Spread pastry with pesto; top with tomatoes and
olives. Sprinkle with cheese. Bake about 10 minutes.
Drizzle with remaining oil before serving.
nutritional count per serving **28.4g total fat
(13.1g saturated fat); 1672kJ (400 cal);
22g carbohydrate; 13.5g protein; 2.9g fibre**

tomato, pesto and olive tart

[**preparation time** 10 minutes **cooking time** 20 minutes **serves** 4]

Cherry tomatoes can be substituted for grape
tomatoes, if you like.
Basil pesto is available, ready-made, from
supermarkets and delicatessens.
If you have some, scatter 2 teaspoons fresh
thyme leaves over the tart just before serving.

Drain the spinach very
thoroughly so that the
moisture does not seep
into the tart base and
make the pastry soggy.

[**preparation time** 10 minutes **cooking time** 20 minutes **serves** 4]

spinach and beetroot tart

1 sheet ready-rolled puff pasty
250g frozen spinach, thawed, drained
1 cup (200g) fetta cheese, crumbled
½ x 850g can drained baby beetroot,
    sliced thinly

1   Preheat oven to 220°C/200°C fan-forced.
2   Place pastry on an oiled oven tray. Fold edges
of pastry over to make a 0.5cm border all the
way around pastry. Prick pastry base with fork.
Place another oven tray on top of pastry; bake
10 minutes. Remove top tray from pastry; reduce
temperature to 200°C/180°C fan-forced.
3   Meanwhile, combine spinach with half the
cheese in medium bowl.
4   Top tart with spinach mixture, beetroot and
remaining cheese. Bake about 10 minutes.
nutritional count per serving **21.4g total fat**
(12.8g saturated fat); 1421kJ (340 cal);
22.1g carbohydrate; 13.4g protein; 4g fibre

[**preparation time** 25 minutes **cooking time** 55 minutes **serves** 6]

spinach and pumpkin fillo pie

We've added pumpkin to the spinach to give a new look to the traditional Greek recipe for spanakopita. You could also make this pie in individual pie dishes.

75g butter, melted
1 tablespoon olive oil
1 medium brown onion (150g), chopped finely
2 cloves garlic, crushed
1kg butternut pumpkin, chopped finely
1 tablespoon brown sugar
1 teaspoon ground cumin
½ teaspoon ground nutmeg
2 x 250g frozen spinach, thawed, drained
1 cup (200g) fetta cheese
2 eggs, beaten lightly
6 sheets fillo pastry

1   Brush 24cm ovenproof pie dish with some of the butter.
2   Heat oil in large frying pan; cook onion and garlic, stirring, until onion softens. Add pumpkin, sugar and spices; cook, covered, about 20 minutes or until pumpkin is tender. Stir in spinach and ¾ cup of the cheese. Remove from heat; cool 5 minutes. Stir in egg.
3   Preheat oven to 180°C/160°C fan-forced.
4   Layer two sheets of pastry, brushing each with butter; fold pastry in half widthways, place in pie dish, edges overhanging. Brush pastry with butter again. Repeat with remaining pastry, overlapping the pieces clockwise around the dish. Fold over edges to make a rim around the edge of the pie; brush with remaining butter. Spoon pumpkin mixture into dish.
5   Bake about 40 minutes or until browned lightly. Sprinkle with remaining cheese.
nutritional count per serving 24.4g total fat (13.4g saturated fat); 1588kJ (380 cal); 23.2g carbohydrate; 15g protein; 5.1g fibre

from the freezer

Don't be caught short wanting a substantial meat meal because you haven't had time to go to the butcher. Beef, veal, lamb, pork, poultry and fish all freeze well, and only need to be thawed in the fridge the night before cooking, for larger cuts, or the day of cooking, for smaller cuts. And don't forget the frozen vegies...they're a life saver for those of us short of time.

chilli lamb stir-fry

[**preparation time** 10 minutes **cooking time** 25 minutes **serves** 4]

Serve stir-fry with steamed rice.
If you like, add some asian greens during the last few minutes of the cooking time. Beef can be used in place of the lamb.

2 tablespoons peanut oil
500g lamb fillets, sliced thinly
4cm piece fresh ginger (20g), sliced thinly
1 large brown onion (200g), sliced thickly
1 large red capsicum (350g), sliced thickly
2 tablespoons water
1 teaspoon dried chilli flakes
2 tablespoons oyster sauce
2 tablespoons light soy sauce

1 Heat half the oil in wok; stir-fry lamb, in batches, until browned.
2 Heat remaining oil in wok; stir-fry ginger, onion and capsicum, 5 minutes. Add the water; cook, covered, about 10 minutes or until vegetables soften.
3 Add chilli and sauces, return lamb to wok; stir-fry, 2 minutes or until heated through.
nutritional count per serving **13.9g total fat (3.7g saturated fat); 1154kJ (276 cal); 8.7g carbohydrate; 28.4g protein; 1.6g fibre**

You need to soak eight bamboo skewers in water for least 20 minutes before using to prevent them from scorching during cooking.

[**preparation time** 25 minutes **cooking time** 20 minutes **serves** 4]

chicken and haloumi skewers with pilaf

2½ cups (625ml) chicken stock
25g butter
1 medium brown onion (150g), chopped finely
1 bay leaf
1⅓ cups (265g) basmati rice, rinsed, drained
600g chicken breast fillets, cut into 2cm pieces
250g haloumi cheese, cut into 16 pieces
8 cherry tomatoes
2 tablespoons olive oil
lemon yogurt sauce
1 cup (280g) greek-style yogurt
½ clove garlic, crushed
1 teaspoon finely grated lemon rind
1 tablespoon lemon juice
2 tablespoons finely chopped fresh flat-leaf parsley

Haloumi is a firm, sheep-milk cheese with a minty, salty flavour; it does not break down when cooked, however, it should be eaten while still warm as it becomes tough and rubbery on cooling.
This recipe is perfect for cooking on the barbecue when entertaining friends or family – serve with a couscous salad for a quick and tasty dinner.

1   Heat stock in small saucepan.
2   To make pilaf, melt butter in large saucepan; cook onion, stirring, until soft. Add bay leaf and rice; cook, stirring, 2 minutes. Add stock; simmer, covered, about 10 minutes or until rice is tender and liquid absorbed.
3   Meanwhile, make lemon yogurt sauce.
4   Thread chicken, cheese and tomatoes alternately onto skewers; brush with oil.
5   Cook skewers on heated oiled grill plate (or grill or barbecue) until chicken is cooked. Serve skewers with pilaf and lemon yogurt sauce.
lemon yogurt sauce Combine ingredients in small bowl.
nutritional count per serving **39.1g total fat (17.7g saturated fat); 3494kJ (836 cal); 63.9g carbohydrate; 56.2g protein; 1.8g fibre**

Creamy mashed potato goes
well with saltimbocca, if you
prefer serving that to
roasted potatoes.
For a truly decadent mash,
stir in ⅔ cup of mascarpone
cheese before serving.

[**preparation time** 15 minutes **cooking time** 35 minutes **serves** 4]

veal saltimbocca with roasted potatoes

6 small potatoes (720g), quartered
2 tablespoons olive oil
4 x 100g veal schnitzels
4 fresh sage leaves
4 rindless middle bacon strips (260g)
15g butter
1 cup (250ml) dry white wine

1   Preheat oven to 240°C/220°C fan-forced.
2   Boil, steam or microwave potato 5 minutes;
drain, pat dry with absorbent paper.
3   Place potato, in single layer, on oven tray;
drizzle with half the oil. Roast 30 minutes.
4   Meanwhile, roll each schnitzel, top with sage
leaves. Wrap bacon around each schnitzel, secure
with toothpicks or small skewers.
5   Heat remaining oil and butter in large frying pan;
cook saltimbocca, bacon seam-side down, turning
occasionally, until cooked. Remove from pan.
6   Pour wine into pan; bring to the boil, stirring.
Boil until liquid is reduced by half. Serve saltimbocca
with potato, drizzled with wine sauce.
nutritional count per serving **17.4g total fat
(5g saturated fat); 1940kJ (464 cal);
24.1g carbohydrate; 40.6g protein; 3.6g fibre**

2 teaspoons ground cumin

2 teaspoons ground ginger

1 teaspoon ground coriander

1 teaspoon dried chilli flakes

5 dried curry leaves

1 tablespoon peanut oil

2 cloves garlic, crushed

1 medium red onion (170g), sliced thinly

2 x 400ml cans coconut milk

2 tablespoons kecap asin

1 tablespoon brown sugar

800g butternut pumpkin, chopped coarsely

600g chicken thigh fillets, chopped coarsely

250g snow peas, trimmed

⅓ cup (80ml) lime juice

⅔ cup (90g) coarsely chopped roasted
   unsalted peanuts

1   Dry-fry spices in wok over medium heat,
stirring, about 1 minute or until fragrant. Add
curry leaves, oil, garlic and onion; stir-fry until
onion softens.

2   Add coconut milk, kecap asin, sugar, pumpkin
and chicken; simmer, uncovered, about 20 minutes
or until pumpkin softens. Remove from heat, stir
in snow peas and juice. Serve sprinkled with nuts.

nutritional count per serving **68.5g total fat**
(42.3g saturated fat); 3900kJ (933 cal);
31.4g carbohydrate; 44.8g protein; 10g fibre

chicken and pumpkin curry

[**preparation time** 25 minutes **cooking time** 35 minutes **serves** 4]

You can add ½ cup
firmly packed fresh
coriander leaves just
before serving. Serve
with steamed rice.

[**preparation time** 20 minutes **cooking time** 1 hour 10 minutes **serves** 4]

jambalaya

This dish is a real one-pot-wonder; very similar to the Spanish staple, paella: jambalaya is the US-version and, like paella, often contains seafood. Jalapeño chillies are fairly hot green chillies, sold finely chopped or whole, bottled in vinegar, as well as fresh from specialty greengrocers; we used the chopped, medium-hot, sweetish bottled version in our recipes.

1 tablespoon olive oil
4 smoked chorizo sausages (680g)
400g chicken breast fillets
1 medium red onion (170g), chopped finely
1 medium red capsicum (200g), chopped finely
2 cloves garlic, crushed
2 tablespoons finely chopped bottled jalapeño chillies
1 teaspoon dried oregano
¼ teaspoon cayenne pepper
1 bay leaf
2 tablespoons tomato paste
1½ cups (300g) white long-grain rice
400g can crushed tomatoes
2 cups (500ml) chicken stock

1 Heat oil in large saucepan; cook sausages, turning occasionally, until browned. Remove from pan; slice thickly. Add chicken to pan; cook, turning occasionally, until browned. Remove from pan; slice thickly.
2 Cook onion, capsicum and garlic in same pan, stirring, until capsicum softens. Add chilli; cook, stirring, 1 minute. Add spices, bay leaf and paste; cook, stirring, 2 minutes. Add rice; stir to coat in mixture.
3 Add undrained tomatoes and stock, bring to a simmer; return sausage and chicken to pan. Cook, covered, about 45 minutes or until rice is tender and liquid absorbed.

nutritional count per serving **62.3g total fat (21.2g saturated fat); 4648kJ (1112 cal); 73g carbohydrate; 63.3g protein; 4.5g fibre**

[**preparation time** 15 minutes (plus standing time) **cooking time** 1 hour 20 minutes **serves** 4]

roast lemon and cumin chicken

¼ cup (60ml) olive oil
2 tablespoons ground cumin
⅓ cup (80ml) lemon juice
2kg whole chicken
1 medium lemon (140g), halved
1 small brown onion (80g), chopped finely
125g cherry tomatoes, halved
250g frozen chopped spinach, thawed, drained
½ cup (125ml) chicken stock
2 x 400g cans white beans, rinsed, drained

You need two lemons
for this recipe.
An easy way to judge
if the chicken is
cooked, is to poke it
with a skewer in the
thickest part, near
where a leg joins the
body – if the juice runs
clear, the chicken
should be cooked; if
the juice runs pink, the
chicken needs longer
in the oven.

1   Preheat oven to 200°C/180°C fan-forced.
2   Combine 2 tablespoons of the oil, 1½ tablespoons of the cumin and 2 tablespoons of the lemon juice in small bowl.
3   Sprinkle cavity of chicken with remaining cumin, place lemon halves in the cavity. Rub skin all over with cumin oil mixture; tie chicken legs together with kitchen string.
4   Half fill a large baking dish with water; place chicken on oiled wire rack over dish. Roast 20 minutes. Reduce temperature to 180°C/160°C fan-forced; roast chicken about 1 hour or until cooked. Remove chicken from rack; cover, stand 20 minutes.
5   Meanwhile, heat remaining oil in large frying pan; cook onion, stirring, until soft. Add tomato; cook, stirring, 2 minutes. Add spinach and stock; cook until liquid is almost evaporated. Add beans; cook, stirring, 1 minute. Remove from heat; stir in remaining juice. Serve roast chicken with warm white bean salad.
nutritional count per serving **51g total fat (13.6g saturated fat); 2909kJ (696 cal); 6.7g carbohydrate; 50.9g protein; 6g fibre**

[**preparation time** 25 minutes **cooking time** 40 minutes **serves** 4]

sumac lamb loin on pearl barley salad

1 clove garlic, crushed
1 tablespoon sumac
2 teaspoons ground coriander
2 tablespoons hot water
8 lamb loin chops (800g)
1 cup (200g) pearl barley
1 small red onion (100g), quartered
1 small red capsicum (150g), sliced thickly
1 small kumara (250g), halved lengthways, sliced thickly
2 tablespoons olive oil
2 tablespoons white wine vinegar
130g firm fetta cheese, crumbled

1 Combine garlic, spices, the water and lamb in medium bowl.
2 Cook barley, uncovered, in large saucepan of boiling water about 30 minutes or until tender; drain. Rinse under cold water; drain.
3 Meanwhile, toss vegetables with half the oil in medium bowl. Cook vegetables on heated oiled grill plate (or grill or barbecue) until onion softens. Remove onion and capsicum; chop coarsely. Cook kumara further 5 minutes; chop coarsely.
4 Meanwhile, cook lamb on heated oiled grill.
5 Combine barley, vegetables, remaining oil and vinegar in medium bowl; sprinkle with cheese. Serve lamb with barley salad.
nutritional count per serving 31.1g total fat (12.8g saturated fat); 2633kJ (630 cal); 40.2g carbohydrate; 43.7g protein; 7.4g fibre

If you have some, stir ⅓ cup coarsely chopped fresh mint into the salad just before serving.
Cook vegetables slowly to prevent them blackening before they have softened.
Before adding lamb to the grill, increase heat to medium-high.

700g beef mince

2 cloves garlic, crushed

1 small brown onion (80g), chopped finely

1 small carrot (70g), grated coarsely

⅓ cup (35g) packaged breadcrumbs

1 egg

4cm piece fresh ginger (20g), chopped finely

2 tablespoons light soy sauce

¼ cup (60ml) hoisin sauce

1 tablespoon peanut oil

4 cups (320g) finely sliced cabbage

1 teaspoon sesame oil

1   Preheat oven to 180°C/160°C fan-forced.

2   Combine beef, garlic, onion, carrot, breadcrumbs, egg, half the ginger, half the soy sauce and 2 tablespoons of the hoisin sauce in large bowl. Press mixture firmly into oiled 14cm x 21cm loaf pan; bake, uncovered, about 45 minutes or until meatloaf shrinks from the sides of the pan.

3   Meanwhile, heat peanut oil in wok; stir-fry remaining ginger. Add cabbage; stir-fry until wilted. Remove from heat; stir in sesame oil.

4   Slice meatloaf; drizzle with combined remaining sauces. Serve with stir-fried cabbage.

nutritional count per serving 20.5g total fat (6.7g saturated fat); 1777kJ (425 cal); 16.4g carbohydrate; 40.9g protein; 6.1g fibre

meatloaf with stir-fried cabbage

You need approximately a third of a small savoy cabbage for this recipe. If you don't have any cabbage, stir-fry any vegetable that takes your fancy – buk choy and gai lan stir-fry particularly well.

[preparation time 15 minutes cooking time 45 minutes serves 4]

[**preparation time** 20 minutes **cooking time** 1 hour 25 minutes **serves** 6]

creamed spinach, kumara and potato gratin

10g butter
1 teaspoon olive oil
1 medium brown onion (150g), chopped finely
2 x 250g packets frozen spinach, thawed, drained
300ml cream
¾ cup (180ml) milk
1 large kumara (500g), sliced thinly
2 large potatoes (600g), sliced thinly
⅓ cup (25g) coarsely grated parmesan cheese

1 Preheat oven to 220°C/200°C fan-forced. Oil deep medium 25cm x 30cm baking dish.
2 Melt butter with oil in medium frying pan, add onion; cook, stirring, until onion softens. Add spinach, ½ cup of the cream and ½ cup of the milk; cook, stirring, 2 minutes.
3 Place a third of the kumara and a third of the potato, slightly overlapping, in dish; spread with half the spinach mixture. Repeat layering, ending with kumara and potato. Pour over remaining combined cream and milk; sprinkle with cheese.
4 Bake, covered, about 1 hour or until potato is tender. Uncover; bake about 10 minutes or until browned lightly.
nutritional count per serving 26.7g total fat (16.9g saturated fat); 1655kJ (396 cal); 27.6g carbohydrate; 9.2g protein; 5.7g fibre

[**preparation time** 20 minutes (plus refrigeration time) **cooking time** 15 minutes **serves** 4]

honey pork cutlets with apple cabbage salad

¼ cup (60ml) light soy sauce
2 tablespoons honey
2 cloves garlic, crushed
2 tablespoons lemon juice
½ teaspoon ground clove
2 tablespoons olive oil
4 x 180g pork cutlets
apple cabbage salad
4 cups (320g) finely sliced cabbage
½ cup (75g) raisins
½ cup (50g) roasted walnuts
1 medium apple (150g), sliced thinly
½ teaspoon caraway seeds
1 tablespoon olive oil
¼ cup (60ml) cider vinegar
1 tablespoon lemon juice

You need approximately a third of a small savoy cabbage for this recipe. If you prefer, you can use pork fillet rather than pork cutlets. Pork is best cooked over a moderate heat. The flavours of the salad benefit greatly from standing at room temperature for at least an hour before serving.

1 Combine sauce, honey, garlic, juice, clove, half the oil and pork in large bowl. Refrigerate, covered, 3 hours or overnight.
2 Make apple cabbage salad.
3 Heat remaining oil in large frying pan; cook drained pork, in batches. Serve with salad.
apple cabbage salad Combine ingredients in large bowl.
nutritional count per serving **7.8g total fat (1.1g saturated fat); 606kJ (145 cal); 9.7g carbohydrate; 8.4g protein; 1.7g fibre**

[**preparation time** 25 minutes **cooking time** 1 hour **serves** 4]

grilled peppercorn steak with paprika potatoes

2 cloves garlic, chopped coarsely
1 teaspoon sea salt
2 teaspoons mixed peppercorns
2 teaspoons worcestershire sauce
⅓ cup (80ml) olive oil
4 rib-eye beef steaks (800g)
2 medium red onions (300g), quartered
20g butter
3 medium potatoes (600g), peeled
2 teaspoons smoked paprika

For nicely crisped potatoes, heat the oven tray before adding the potatoes.

1 Preheat oven to 220°C/200°C fan-forced.
2 Using mortar and pestle or blender, grind garlic, salt and peppercorns until smooth; stir in sauce and half of the oil. Rub beef with paste; cover, refrigerate.
3 Enclose four onion quarters and half the butter in aluminium foil. Repeat with remaining onion and butter. Place on oven tray; roast 1 hour.
4 Meanwhile, boil, steam or microwave potatoes 5 minutes; drain. Slice potatoes thickly. Toss with remaining oil and paprika; cook on heated oiled grill plate (or grill or barbecue) until browned.
5 Cook beef on heated oiled grill plate (or grill or barbecue); cover, stand 5 minutes. Serve with buttered onions and paprika potatoes.
nutritional count per serving **34.7g total fat (10.3g saturated fat); 2487kJ (595 cal); 22.6g carbohydrate; 46.7g protein; 3.6g fibre**

If you have some, top the soup with fresh mint leaves. Garlic-and-lemon-rubbed grilled bread or pappadums would make excellent accompaniments for this soup.

[**preparation time** 10 minutes (plus cooling time) **cooking time** 15 minutes **serves** 4]

curried pea soup

10g butter
1 tablespoon olive oil
1 medium brown onion (150g), chopped coarsely
2 tablespoons tikka masala curry paste
1kg frozen peas
3 cups (750ml) chicken stock
1 cup (250ml) water
½ cup (140g) yogurt

1   Melt butter with oil in large saucepan; cook onion, stirring, about 5 minutes or until soft.
2   Add paste to onion mixture; cook, stirring, until fragrant. Add peas, stock and the water; bring to the boil. Reduce heat, simmer, uncovered, 5 minutes. Cool 15 minutes.
3   Blend or process soup, in batches, with yogurt, until smooth. Return soup to pan, stir until heated through.

nutritional count per serving **13.2g total fat (3.5g saturated fat); 1333kJ (319 cal); 24.7g carbohydrate; 16.9g protein; 17.9g fibre**

1½ cups (300g) jasmine rice
2 x 400ml cans coconut milk
3cm piece fresh ginger (15g), sliced thinly
1 clove garlic, sliced thinly
1 tablespoon fish sauce
1 tablespoon brown sugar
2 teaspoons sambal oelek
4 x 180g firm white fish fillets
250g frozen spinach, thawed, drained
2 tablespoons lime juice
2 green onions, sliced
2 tablespoons fried shallots

1 Cook rice in large saucepan of boiling water, uncovered, until tender; drain.
2 Meanwhile, combine coconut milk, ginger, garlic, sauce, sugar and sambal in large frying pan; bring to the boil. Reduce heat; simmer, uncovered, 10 minutes. Add fish; simmer, covered, about 10 minutes or until fish is cooked. Remove fish from pan.
3 Add spinach and juice to pan; cook, stirring, until hot. Serve fish with coconut spinach and rice; sprinkle over green onion and fried shallots.
nutritional count per serving 46.6g total fat (37.7g saturated fat); 3795kJ (908 cal); 71.9g carbohydrate; 47.5g protein; 6.2g fibre

coconut-poached fish with spinach

[preparation time 10 minutes cooking time 25 minutes serves 4]

Chicken can be used in place of the fish.

You can use any firm
white fish fillet you
like in this recipe, for
example, blue-eye,
ling or snapper.

[**preparation time** 20 minutes **cooking time** 40 minutes **serves** 4]

creamy fish pie

10g butter
2 teaspoons olive oil
1 small brown onion (80g), chopped finely
1 medium carrot (120g), chopped finely
1 trimmed celery stalk (100g), chopped finely
1 tablespoon plain flour
1 cup (250ml) fish stock
500g firm white fish fillets, chopped coarsely
½ cup (125ml) cream
1 tablespoon english mustard
1 cup (120g) frozen peas
½ cup (40g) finely grated parmesan cheese
1 sheet ready-rolled puff pastry
1 egg, beaten lightly

You can stir ¼ cup coarsely
chopped fresh flat-leaf parsley
into the mixture when adding
the fish.
It is important you use a shallow
baking dish so that the top of the
fish mixture is touching the
pastry and the pastry is not stuck
to the sides of the dish, as this
could prevent it from rising.

1   Preheat oven to 220°C/200°C fan-forced.
2   Melt butter with oil in large saucepan; cook onion, carrot and celery,
stirring, until carrot softens. Stir in flour; cook, stirring, 2 minutes. Add stock
and fish; cook, stirring, until fish is cooked through and mixture boils and
thickens. Remove from heat; stir in cream, mustard, peas and cheese.
3   Spoon mixture into a shallow small 1.5 litre (6-cup) baking dish; top with
pastry. Brush top with egg. Bake about 20 minutes or until browned.
nutritional count per serving **35.1g total fat (19.1g saturated fat); 2366kJ**
(566 cal); 23.5g carbohydrate; 37.5g protein; 4.1g fibre

sweet endings

You can never count on when the hungry hordes will want dessert or a sweet snack. The recipes in this chapter can be magically concocted with ingredients from the pantry or the freezer and will wow the crowd every time. Keep canned fruit, ice-cream or dried goods on hand to keep sweet cravings at bay.

poached pears with chocolate sauce

[**preparation time** 15 minutes (plus cooling time) **cooking time** 45 minutes **serves** 4]

If you can't find corella pears, use four beurre bosc pears instead. The same quantity of red wine can be used in place of the port; the end result may not be as sweet, so adjust sweetening accordingly.
Pears can be reheated gently in the syrup, or served cold.
You can sprinkle some fine strips of orange rind over the pears to serve.

1.5 litres (6 cups) water
2 cups (500ml) port
½ cup (110g) caster sugar
2 x 8cm strips orange rind
2 tablespoons orange juice
8 corella pears (480g), peeled
¼ cup (60ml) cream
75g milk eating chocolate, chopped coarsely

1   Combine the water, port, sugar, rind and juice in large saucepan. Add pears; bring to the boil. Reduce heat; simmer, covered, about 20 minutes or until pears are tender. Cool pears in syrup.
2   Remove pears from syrup; strain syrup into medium heatproof bowl. Return 2 cups of the strained syrup to same pan (discard remaining syrup); bring to the boil. Boil, uncovered, about 15 minutes or until syrup is reduced to about ½ cup; stir in cream, simmer until slightly thickened. Add chocolate, stir until smooth. Serve pears with chocolate sauce.
nutritional count per serving **11.7g total fat (7.4g saturated fat); 2182kJ (522 cal); 69.4g carbohydrate; 2.4g protein; 1.9g fibre**

[**preparation time** 10 minutes **cooking time** 40 minutes **serves** 6]

berry frangipane tart

Frangipane is a delicious
almond-flavoured filling for
pies, tarts and cakes.
We've used mixed berries in
this recipe, however, you can
use any berries you like. It is
important to used frozen berries
to prevent the colour bleeding
dramatically through the
frangipane as it cooks.

1 sheet ready-rolled sweet puff pastry
300g frozen mixed berries
frangipane
80g butter, softened
½ teaspoon vanilla extract
⅓ cup (75g) caster sugar
2 egg yolks
1 tablespoon plain flour
1 cup (120g) almond meal

1   Preheat oven to 220°C/200°C fan-forced. Grease 20cm x 30cm
lamington pan.
2   Roll pastry until large enough to cover base and sides of pan; line pan
with pastry, press into sides. Prick pastry all over with fork; freeze 5 minutes.
3   Place another lamington pan on top of pastry; bake 5 minutes. Remove
top pan; bake about 5 minutes or until pastry is browned lightly. Cool
5 minutes. Reduce temperature to 180°C/160°C fan-forced.
4   Meanwhile, make frangipane.
5   Spread frangipane over pastry base. Sprinkle with berries, press into
frangipane. Bake about 30 minutes or until browned lightly.
frangipane   Beat butter, extract, sugar and egg yolks in small bowl with
electric mixer until light and fluffy. Stir in flour and almond meal.
nutritional count per serving   **30.2g total fat (11.9g saturated fat); 1722kJ
(412 cal); 26.4g carbohydrate; 7.7g protein; 3.3g fibre**

10g butter, softened
1 tablespoon caster sugar
2 eggs, separated
170g can passionfruit in syrup
²/₃ cup (110g) icing sugar
4 egg whites
1 tablespoon icing sugar, extra, for dusting

1   Preheat oven to 220°C/200°C fan-forced. Grease four 1-cup (250ml) soufflé dishes with butter; sprinkle with caster sugar, shake away excess.
2   Combine egg yolks, passionfruit and half the sifted icing sugar in large bowl.
3   Beat egg whites in small bowl with electric mixer until soft peaks form; add remaining sifted icing sugar, beat until firm peaks form. Gently fold a third of the egg white mixture into passionfruit mixture, then fold in remaining egg white mixture.
4   Place dishes on oven tray. Spoon soufflé mixture into dishes; bake about 12 minutes or until soufflés are puffed and golden. Dust with extra sifted icing sugar; serve immediately.

nutritional count per soufflé 4.8g total fat (2.2g saturated fat); 995kJ (238 cal); 37.3g carbohydrate; 8.2g protein; 5.9g fibre

passionfruit soufflés

[**preparation time** 10 minutes **cooking time** 12 minutes **makes** 4]

The word soufflé is derived from the French verb "souffler", which means to "blow up" – when you see your soufflés magically rise in the oven, you'll understand exactly why it has the name it does.

If you prefer milk chocolate, it can be substituted for the dark chocolate. Top with a few extra cherries for decoration.

[**preparation time** 10 minutes (plus cooling and refrigeration time) **cooking time** 5 minutes **serves** 6]

choc-cherry mascarpone cream

425g can sour cherries in syrup
300ml thickened cream
1 tablespoon caster sugar
200g dark eating chocolate, chopped coarsely
250g mascarpone cheese

1 Drain cherries, reserve ¼ cup of syrup.
2 Bring cream, sugar and reserved syrup to the boil. Remove from heat; add chocolate, stir until smooth. Cool.
3 Place cheese in small bowl of electric mixer; add chocolate mixture, beat until smooth.
4 Divide cherries between six ¾-cup (180ml) dishes; top with chocolate mixture. Pudding can be served immediately or refrigerated for about 30 minutes to set.

nutritional count per serving **52g total fat (33.6g saturated fat); 2558kJ (612 cal); 33.4g carbohydrate; 3.7g protein; 1.1g fibre**

[**preparation time** 20 minutes **cooking time** 35 minutes **serves** 6]

cinnamon almond cake

¼ cup (40g) roasted almonds
½ cup (125ml) milk
80g butter, softened
1 teaspoon vanilla extract
½ cup (110g) firmly packed brown sugar
2 eggs
1 cup (150g) self-raising flour
2 teaspoons ground cinnamon
20g butter, melted
nut topping
½ cup (80g) blanched almonds, chopped finely
¼ cup (40g) icing sugar
1 teaspoon ground cinnamon

1 Preheat oven to 180°C/160°C fan-forced. Grease 8cm x 26cm bar cake pan; line base with baking paper, extending paper 5cm above long sides of pan.
2 Blend or process nuts until chopped coarsely; add milk, process until smooth.
3 Beat softened butter, extract and sugar in small bowl with electric mixer until light and fluffy. Beat in eggs, one at a time (mixture may separate at this stage, but will come together later).
4 Stir in sifted flour, cinnamon and almond mixture. Pour into pan; bake about 35 minutes. Stand cake in pan 10 minutes before turning, top-side up, onto wire rack to cool.
5 Increase temperature to 200°C/180°C fan-forced.
6 Meanwhile, make nut topping.
7 Brush cake with melted butter; sprinkle with nut topping.
nut topping Place nuts in strainer; rinse under cold water. Combine wet nuts in small bowl with sifted icing sugar and cinnamon; spread mixture onto oven tray, roast about 10 minutes or until nuts are dry.
nutritional count per serving 27.7g total fat (10.8g saturated fat); 1956kJ (468 cal); 44g carbohydrate; 9.6g protein; 2.8g fibre

Rather than cooking all the cookie dough, stir some of the raw mixture through ice-cream for the ultimate cookie-dough ice-cream.

[**preparation time** 15 minutes **cooking time** 10 minutes **makes** 28]

peanut butter choc-chunk cookies

75g butter, softened
1 teaspoon vanilla extract
¼ cup (55g) caster sugar
¼ cup (55g) firmly packed brown sugar
⅔ cup (190g) smooth peanut butter
1 egg
1 cup (150g) plain flour
½ teaspoon bicarbonate of soda
150g milk eating chocolate, chopped coarsely

1 Preheat oven to 180°C/160°C fan-forced. Grease two oven trays; line with baking paper.
2 Beat butter, extract and sugars in small bowl with electric mixer until smooth. Add peanut butter; beat until combined. Add egg; beat until combined. Stir in sifted flour and soda, then chocolate.
3 Drop level tablespoons of mixture, about 5cm apart, onto trays; press down slightly to flatten. Bake about 10 minutes or until beginning to brown; cool cookies on trays.
nutritional count per cookie **7.3g total fat (3g saturated fat); 531kJ (127 cal); 11.7g carbohydrate; 3.1g protein; 1g fibre**

1 cup (150g) plain flour
½ cup (75g) self-raising flour
1 cup (220g) caster sugar
⅔ cup (50g) desiccated coconut
75g butter, melted
2 eggs, beaten lightly
1 teaspoon coconut extract
1 cup (250ml) buttermilk

1   Preheat oven to 180°C/160°C fan-forced.
Grease 14cm x 21cm loaf pan; line base with
baking paper, extending paper 5cm above long
sides of pan.
2   Sift flours into medium bowl; stir in sugar
and coconut.
3   Add butter, egg, extract and buttermilk to flour
mixture, stir until combined; pour into pan.
4   Bake about 1 hour. Stand loaf in pan 10 minutes
before turning, top-side up, onto wire rack to cool.
nutritional count per serving 14.1g total fat
(9.5g saturated fat); 1492kJ (357 cal);
49.9g carbohydrate; 6.4g protein; 2g fibre

coconut bread

[preparation time 10 minutes cooking time 1 hour serves 8]

A delicious breakfast can be prepared in a
flash with this coconut bread – just pop it
under the grill for a couple of minutes until
it begins to brown lightly and, if you like,
spread it with a little butter. This bread
freezes well, so you can always slice it,
wrap it well in plastic wrap, and freeze it
in an air-tight container; thaw it out or
toast it as you need it.

[**preparation time** 30 minutes **cooking time** 20 minutes **makes** 18]

apple cranberry turnovers

It's important to serve the turnovers as soon as they come out of the oven, due to the delicate nature of the fillo pastry.
Serve turnovers dusted with sifted icing sugar for a delicious mid-afternoon treat or, for a yummy dessert, serve with ice-cream.

40g butter
4 medium apples (600g), peeled, chopped finely
¼ cup (55g) firmly packed brown sugar
⅓ cup (45g) dried cranberries
⅓ cup (35g) coarsely chopped roasted walnuts
1 teaspoon ground cinnamon
2 teaspoons lemon juice
12 sheets fillo pastry
75g butter, melted

1   Melt butter in large frying pan, add apple; cook, stirring, about 10 minutes or until apple is tender. Add sugar; stir until dissolved. Remove from heat, stir in cranberries, nuts, cinnamon and juice. Cool.
2   Preheat oven to 220°C/200°C fan-forced. Grease oven trays.
3   Place four sheets of pastry on top of each other; cover remaining sheets with baking paper then a damp tea towel. Cut six 12cm rounds from pastry. Brush between each layer of pastry with some of the melted butter.
4   Repeat step 3 with remaining sheets (you will have 18 pastry rounds).
5   Divide apple mixture among pastry rounds. Fold over pastry to enclose filling, pressing edges together. Brush turnovers with remaining butter.
6   Bake about 8 minutes or until browned lightly.
nutritional count per turnover **6.8g total fat (3.6g saturated fat); 497kJ (119 cal); 12.7g carbohydrate; 1.4g protein; 0.9g fibre**

1 litre (4 cups) milk
300ml cream
1 cup (200g) arborio rice
½ cup (110g) caster sugar
½ teaspoon ground cardamom
½ teaspoon ground cinnamon
¾ cup (110g) raisins
caramelised apples
40g butter
¼ cup (55g) firmly packed brown sugar
2 medium apples (300g), peeled,
    cored, quartered

1   Combine milk, cream, rice and sugar in large
saucepan; stir over heat, without boiling, until
sugar dissolves. Bring to the boil; reduce heat.
Cook, stirring, about 20 minutes or until rice
is tender.
2   Meanwhile, make caramelised apples.
3   Stir in spices and raisins; cook, stirring,
5 minutes. Serve rice pudding topped with apples.
caramelised apples Melt butter in small
saucepan; stir in sugar and apples. Stir over
low heat about 10 minutes or until sauce is
thickened and apples are tender.
nutritional count per serving 51g total fat
(33.4g saturated fat); 4193kJ (1003 cal);
120g carbohydrate; 14.1g protein; 2.7g fibre

rice pudding with cardamom and raisins

[**preparation time** 5 minutes **cooking time** 25 minutes **serves** 4]

You can use any dried fruit in place of the raisins in this recipe, for example, dried apricot or peach.

These tarts must be served warm to be enjoyed at their best. Serve with a good dollop of cream, if you like.

[**preparation time** 15 minutes **cooking time** 15 minutes **makes** 6]

sticky pecan tarts

3 sheets ready-rolled puff pastry
cooking-oil spray
60g butter
2 tablespoons brown sugar
2 tablespoons light corn syrup
1 tablespoon maple syrup
1 cup (120g) roasted pecans
⅓ cup (25g) shredded coconut, toasted
1 teaspoon ground nutmeg

1   Preheat oven to 220°C/200°C fan-forced. Grease 12-hole (⅓-cup/80ml) muffin pan.
2   Cut twelve 8cm rounds from pastry. Place rounds in pan holes; prick bases with fork, spray with cooking-oil spray. Top with another muffin pan; bake 5 minutes. Remove top pan; bake 2 minutes.
3   Meanwhile, combine butter, sugar and syrups in medium saucepan; cook, stirring, without boiling, until sugar dissolves. Bring to a simmer; cook 5 minutes. Stir in nuts, coconut and nutmeg.
4   Divide pecan mixture among pastry cases; bake in oven about 5 minutes.
nutritional count per tart **44.9g total fat (18.9g saturated fat); 2579kJ (617 cal); 45.5g carbohydrate; 7g protein; 3.4g fibre**

glossary

ALLSPICE also known as pimento or jamaican pepper; so-named because it tastes like a combination of nutmeg, cumin, clove and cinnamon – all spices.

ANGEL HAIR PASTA also known as barbina. Long, thin, delicate strands of spaghetti-like pasta; is called "capelli d'angelo" in Italian.

ARTICHOKES
globe large flower-bud of a member of the thistle family; it has tough petal-like leaves, and is edible in part when cooked.
hearts the tender centre of the globe artichoke; can be harvested from the plant after the prickly choke is removed. Buy from delicatessens or canned in brine.
jerusalem neither from Jerusalem nor an artichoke, this crunchy brown-skinned tuber tastes a bit like a water chestnut and belongs to the sunflower family. Eat raw in salads or cooked like potatoes.

BACON, STREAKY from the belly of the pig. Comes in strips with long veins of fat running parallel to the rind.

BAMBOO SHOOTS the tender shoots of bamboo plants, available in cans; must be drained and rinsed before use.

BASIL
sweet the most common type of basil; used extensively in Italian dishes and one of the main ingredients in pesto.
thai also known as horapa; different from sweet basil in both look and taste, having smaller leaves, purplish stems and a slight aniseed taste.

BEANS
broad also known as fava, windsor and horse beans; available dried, fresh, canned and frozen. Fresh and frozen beans should be peeled twice (discarding both the outer long green pod and the beige-green tough inner shell) before using.
kidney medium-sized red bean, slightly floury in texture yet sweet in flavour; sold dried or canned. It's found in bean mixes and is the bean used in chilli con carne.
sprouts also known as bean shoots; tender new growths of assorted beans and seeds germinated for consumption as sprouts. The most readily available are alfalfa, mung beans, soy beans and snow pea sprouts.

white in this book, some recipes may simply call for "white beans", a generic term we use for canned or dried cannellini, haricot, navy or great northern beans.

BICARBONATE OF SODA also known as baking or carb soda; used as a leavening agent in baking.

BUK CHOY also known as bok choy, pak choi, chinese white cabbage or chinese chard; has a fresh, mild mustard taste. Use both stems and leaves. Baby buk choy, also known as pak kat farang or shanghai bok choy, is smaller and more tender than buk choy.

BUTTERMILK originally the term given to the slightly sour liquid left after butter was churned from cream, today it is made similarly to yogurt. Despite the implication of its name, it is low in fat. Sold alongside fresh milk products in supermarkets.

CAPERS the grey-green buds of a warm climate (usually Mediterranean) shrub, sold either dried and salted or pickled in a vinegar brine. Tiny young ones, called baby capers, are also available both in brine or dried in salt.

CAPSICUM also known as pepper or bell pepper. Native to Central and South America; found in red, green, yellow, orange or purplish-black varieties. Seeds and membranes should be discarded before use.

CARDAMOM a spice native to India and used extensively in its cuisine; can be purchased in pod, seed or ground form. Has a distinctive aromatic, sweetly rich flavour and is one of the world's most expensive spices.

CHEESE
cheddar a semi-hard cows-milk cheese. It ranges in colour from white to pale yellow, and has a slightly crumbly texture if properly matured. The flavour becomes sharper with time.
fetta salty, white cheese with a milky, fresh acidity. Most commonly made from cows' milk, although sheep and goat varieties are also available.
haloumi a firm, cream-coloured sheep-milk cheese matured in brine; somewhat like a minty, salty fetta in flavour. It can be grilled or fried, briefly, without breaking down.

mascarpone a fresh, unripened, smooth, triple cream cheese with a rich, slightly tangy taste. Is whitish to creamy yellow in colour and has a soft, creamy texture.
parmesan also known as parmigiano; is a hard, grainy cows-milk cheese. The curd is salted in brine for a month before being aged for up to two years in humid conditions.
ricotta is a sweet, white, moist cows-milk cheese; the name roughly translates as "cooked again". It's made from whey, a by-product of other cheese-making, to which fresh milk and acid are added.

CHICKPEAS also called garbanzos, channa or hummus; an irregularly round, sandy-coloured legume.

CHINESE COOKING WINE also known as hao hsing or chinese rice wine; made from fermented rice, wheat, sugar and salt. Found in Asian food shops; if you can't find it, you can use mirin or sherry.

CHORIZO SAUSAGE made of coarsely ground pork and highly seasoned with garlic, chilli powder and other spices. It's widely used in both Mexican and Spanish cookery. Mexican chorizo is made with fresh pork, while the Spanish version uses smoked pork.

COCONUT
desiccated unsweetened, concentrated, dried, finely shredded coconut.
shredded thin strips of dried coconut.

CORIANDER also known as pak chee, cilantro or chinese parsley; bright-green leafy herb with a pungent flavour. Both the stems and roots of coriander are also used in Thai cooking; wash well before using. Coriander seeds are also available, ground or whole, but are no substitute for fresh coriander, as the taste is very different.

CORNICHON French for gherkin; a very small variety of cucumber.

COUSCOUS a fine, grain-like cereal product made from semolina; it is rehydrated by steaming, or with the addition of a warm liquid, and swells to three or four times its original size.

DRIED CRANBERRIES dried sweetened cranberries that can be used similarly to any dried fruit.

FILLO PASTRY also known as filo or phyllo; tissue-thin pastry sheets purchased chilled or frozen.

GARAM MASALA a blend of spices based on varying proportions of cardamom, cloves, cinnamon, coriander, fennel and cumin, roasted and ground together. Black pepper and chilli can be added for a hotter version.

GRAPE TOMATO about the size of a grape; they can be oblong, pear or grape-shaped and are often used whole in salads or eaten as a snack.

KALAMATA OLIVES small, sharp-tasting, brine-cured black olives.

KITCHEN STRING made of a natural product such as cotton or hemp so that it neither affects the flavour of the food it's tied around nor melts when heated.

LAMINGTON PAN 20cm x 30cm slab cake pan, 3cm deep.

LEBANESE CUCUMBER short, slender and thin-skinned. Probably the most popular variety because of its tender, edible skin, tiny, yielding seeds and sweet, fresh and flavoursome taste.

LETTUCE
butter small, round, loosely formed heads with a sweet flavour; soft, buttery-textured leaves range from pale green on the outer leaves to pale yellow-green inner leaves.
coral very curly and tightly furled leaves that look like coral; comes in distinctive tasting red and green leaves.
cos also known as romaine lettuce; the traditional caesar salad lettuce. Long, with leaves ranging from dark green on the outside to almost white near the core; the leaves have a stiff centre rib that gives a slight cupping effect to the leaf.
iceberg a heavy, firm round lettuce with tightly packed leaves and a crisp texture; the most common "family" lettuce used on sandwiches and in salads.
mesclun pronounced mess-kluhn; also known as mixed greens or spring salad mix. A blend of assorted young lettuce and other green leaves, including baby spinach leaves, mizuna and curly endive.
mixed baby very similar to mesclun with the exception that only the very youngest, smallest leaves are used in the mix.

mizuna Japanese in origin; frizzy green salad leaves with a delicate mustard flavour.
oak-leaf also known as feuille de chene; curly-leafed but not as frizzy as coral lettuce. Found in both red and green varieties.
radicchio Italian in origin; a member of the chicory family. The dark burgundy leaves have a strong, bitter flavour, and can be cooked or eaten raw in salads.

MUSHROOMS
button small, cultivated white mushrooms with a mild flavour. If a recipe calls for an unspecified type of mushroom, use button.
flat large, flat mushrooms with a rich earthy flavour, ideal for filling and barbecuing. They are sometimes misnamed field mushrooms, which are wild mushrooms.
oyster also known as abalone mushrooms; grey-white mushroom shaped like a fan. Prized for their smooth texture and subtle, oyster-like flavour.
shiitake when fresh are known as chinese black, forest or golden oak mushrooms; although cultivated they have the earthiness and taste of wild mushrooms. Are large and meaty. When dried, they are known as donko or dried chinese mushrooms; rehydrate before use.
swiss brown also known as cremini or roman mushrooms, are light brown mushrooms having a full-bodied flavour. Button or cup mushrooms can be substituted. The large variety are often known as portobello mushrooms.

MUSTARD
american-style a sweet mustard containing mustard seeds, sugar, salt, spices and garlic.
dijon a pale brown, distinctively flavoured, fairly mild french mustard.
english an extremely-hot powdered mustard containing ground mustard seeds (both black or brown and yellow-white), wheat flour and turmeric. Also available in a milder, less hot, version.
wholegrain also known as seeded mustard. A french-style coarse-grain mustard made from crushed mustard seeds and dijon-style french mustard.

NOODLES
dried rice also known as rice stick noodles. Made from rice flour and water; available flat and wide or very thin (vermicelli).

fresh egg also known as ba mee or yellow noodles; made from wheat flour and eggs, sold fresh or dried. Range in size from very fine strands to wide, spaghetti-like pieces as thick as a shoelace.
fresh rice also known as ho fun, khao pun, sen yau, pho or kway tiau. Purchase in strands of various widths or large sheets weighing about 500g, which are then cut into the noodle width desired.
fried crispy egg noodles that have been deep-fried then packaged for sale on supermarket shelves.
hokkien also known as stir-fry noodles; fresh wheat noodles resembling thick, yellow-brown spaghetti.
rice stick also known as sen lek, ho fun or kway teow. They come in different widths; thin used in soups, wide used in stir-fries.
rice vermicelli also known as sen mee, mei fun or bee hoon. Used throughout Asia in spring rolls; made with rice flour.
singapore pre-cooked wheat noodles best described as a thinner version of hokkien; sold, packaged, in the refrigerated section of supermarkets.
soba thin, pale-brown noodle originally from Japan; made from buckwheat and varying proportions of wheat flour. Available dried and fresh.
udon available fresh and dried; broad, white, Japanese wheat noodles similar to the ones used in home-made chicken noodle soup.

OCEAN TROUT a farmed fish with pink, soft flesh. It is from the same family as the atlantic salmon; one can be substituted for the other. Available fresh or smoked.

OIL
cooking spray we use a cholesterol-free cooking spray made from canola oil.
olive made from ripened olives. Extra virgin and virgin are the best, while extra light or light refers to taste not fat levels.
peanut pressed from ground peanuts; most commonly used oil in Asian cooking as it has a high smoke point (capacity to handle high heat without burning).
sesame made from roasted, crushed, white sesame seeds; a flavouring rather than a cooking medium.
vegetable sourced from plants rather than animal fats.

ONIONS
brown and white are interchangeable.
green also known as scallion or, incorrectly, shallot; an immature onion picked before the bulb has formed, having a long, bright-green edible stalk.
red also known as spanish, red spanish or bermuda onion; a sweet-flavoured, large, purple-red onion.
spring crisp, narrow green-leafed tops and a round sweet white bulb larger than green onions.

PAPRIKA ground dried sweet red capsicum (bell pepper); there are many grades and types available including sweet, hot, mild and smoked.

PEARL BARLEY has had its outer husk (bran) removed and been steamed and polished, like rice, before being used in cooking.

PITTA (pita) also known as lebanese bread, a wheat-flour pocket bread sold in large, flat pieces that separate easily into two thin rounds. Also available in small thick pieces called pocket pitta.

POLENTA also known as cornmeal; a flour-like cereal made of dried corn (maize) sold ground in different textures. Also the name of the dish made from it.

PRESERVED LEMON RIND lemons are quartered and preserved in salt and lemon juice. To use, remove and discard the pulp, squeeze juice from rind then rinse well and slice thinly. Available from delicatessens and major supermarkets; once opened, store under refrigeration.

RED CURRY PASTE a hot blend of dried red chillies, onions, garlic, oil, lemon rind, shrimp paste, ground cumin, paprika, ground turmeric and ground black pepper.

RICE
arborio small round-grain rice, well suited to absorb a large amount of liquid; especially good in risottos.
basmati a white, fragrant long-grained rice. Wash several times before cooking.
calrose an extremely versatile medium-grain rice; can be substituted for short- or long-grain rices if necessary.
jasmine fragrant long-grained rice; white rice, either long- or short-grain, can be substituted, but will not taste the same.

long-grain elongated grains that remain separate when cooked; this is the most popular steaming rice in Asia.
short-grain fat, almost round grain with a high starch content; tends to clump together when cooked.

RICE VERMICELLI also known as sen mee, mei fun or bee hoon. Long thin noodles made with rice flour.

RISONI small rice-shape pasta; very similar to another small pasta, orzo.

ROCKET also known as arugula, rugula and rucola; a peppery green leaf. Baby rocket leaves are smaller and less peppery.

SAUCES
fish also called nam pla or nuoc nam; made from pulverised salted fermented fish, most often anchovies. Has a pungent smell and strong taste, so use sparingly.
hoisin a thick, sweet and spicy Chinese paste made from salted fermented soy beans, onions and garlic.
soy made from fermented soy beans. Several variations are available in most supermarkets and Asian food stores.
kecap asin a thick and salty dark soy sauce.
light soy a fairly thin, pale and salty soy sauce; used in dishes in which the natural colour of the ingredients is to be maintained. Not to be confused with salt-reduced or low-sodium soy sauces.
Tabasco brand name of an extremely fiery sauce made from vinegar, thai red chillies and salt.
worcestershire a thin, dark-coloured sauce made from garlic, soy sauce, tamarind, onions, molasses, lime, anchovies, vinegar and other seasonings.

SHALLOTS also called french shallots, golden shallots or eschalots; small, brown-skinned members of the onion family.

SPLIT PEAS a variety of yellow or green pea grown specifically for drying. When dried, the peas usually split along a natural seam. Whole and split dried peas are available in supermarkets and health-food stores.

SUMAC a purple-red, astringent spice ground from berries growing on shrubs that flourish wild around the Mediterranean; adds a tart, lemony flavour to dips and dressings and goes well with barbecued meat.

SYRUP
corn a thick, sweet syrup created by processing cornstarch; comes in light or dark forms. Light corn syrup has been clarified to remove all colour and cloudiness; dark corn syrup, which has caramel flavour and colouring added, has a deeper colour and stronger flavour. Used as a sweetener.
maple a thin syrup distilled from the sap of the maple tree. Maple-flavoured syrup or pancake syrup is not an adequate substitute for the real thing.

TORTILLAS thin, round unleavened bread; purchase frozen, fresh or vacuum-packed. Two kinds are available, one made from wheat flour and the other from corn.

VANILLA
bean dried, long, thin pod from a tropical orchid; the minuscule black seeds inside are used to impart a luscious vanilla flavour in baking and desserts.
extract obtained from vanilla beans infused in water; a non-alcoholic version of essence.

VINEGAR
balsamic made from the juice of Trebbiano grapes; is a deep rich brown colour with a sweet and sour flavour; originally from Modena, Italy, there are now many balsamic vinegars on the market ranging in pungency and quality depending on how long they have been aged. Quality can be determined up to a point by price; use the most expensive sparingly.
cider made from fermented apples.
red wine based on fermented red wine.
rice a colourless vinegar made from fermented rice and flavoured with sugar and salt. Also known as seasoned rice vinegar; sherry can be substituted.
white made from spirit of cane sugar.
white wine made from white wine.

WOMBOK also known as peking cabbage, chinese cabbage or petsai. Elongated in shape with pale green, crinkly leaves, this is the most common cabbage in South-East Asian cooking; can be shredded or chopped and eaten raw, braised, steamed or added to a stir-fry.

ZUCCHINI also known as courgette; small, pale- or dark-green, yellow or white vegetable belonging to the squash family.

conversion chart

MEASURES

One Australian metric measuring cup holds approximately 250ml; one Australian metric tablespoon holds 20ml; one Australian metric teaspoon holds 5ml.

The difference between one country's measuring cups and another's is within a two- or three-teaspoon variance, and will not affect your cooking results. North America, New Zealand and the United Kingdom use a 15ml tablespoon.

All cup and spoon measurements are level. The most accurate way of measuring dry ingredients is to weigh them. When measuring liquids, use a clear glass or plastic jug with the metric markings.

We use large eggs with an average weight of 60g.

DRY MEASURES

METRIC	IMPERIAL
15g	½oz
30g	1oz
60g	2oz
90g	3oz
125g	4oz (¼lb)
155g	5oz
185g	6oz
220g	7oz
250g	8oz (½lb)
280g	9oz
315g	10oz
345g	11oz
375g	12oz (¾lb)
410g	13oz
440g	14oz
470g	15oz
500g	16oz (1lb)
750g	24oz (1½lb)
1kg	32oz (2lb)

LIQUID MEASURES

METRIC	IMPERIAL
30ml	1 fluid oz
60ml	2 fluid oz
100ml	3 fluid oz
125ml	4 fluid oz
150ml	5 fluid oz (¼ pint/1 gill)
190ml	6 fluid oz
250ml	8 fluid oz
300ml	10 fluid oz (½ pint)
500ml	16 fluid oz
600ml	20 fluid oz (1 pint)
1000ml (1 litre)	1¾ pints

LENGTH MEASURES

METRIC	IMPERIAL
3mm	⅛in
6mm	¼in
1cm	½in
2cm	¾in
2.5cm	1in
5cm	2in
6cm	2½in
8cm	3in
10cm	4in
13cm	5in
15cm	6in
18cm	7in
20cm	8in
23cm	9in
25cm	10in
28cm	11in
30cm	12in (1ft)

OVEN TEMPERATURES

These oven temperatures are only a guide for conventional ovens.
For fan-forced ovens, check the manufacturer's manual.

	°C (CELSIUS)	°F (FAHRENHEIT)	GAS MARK
Very slow	120	250	½
Slow	150	275-300	1-2
Moderately slow	160	325	3
Moderate	180	350-375	4-5
Moderately hot	200	400	6
Hot	220	425-450	7-8
Very hot	240	475	9

index

ARE YOU MISSING SOME COOKBOOKS?

The Australian Women's Weekly Cookbooks are available from bookshops, cookshops, supermarkets and other stores all over the world. You can also buy direct from the publisher, using the order form below.

TITLE	RRP	QTY	TITLE	RRP	QTY
100 Fast Fillets	£6.99		Grills	£6.99	
A Taste of Chocolate	£6.99		Healthy Heart Cookbook	£6.99	
After Work Fast	£6.99		Indian Cooking Class	£6.99	
Beginners Cooking Class	£6.99		Japanese Cooking Class	£6.99	
Beginners Thai	£6.99		Just For One	£6.99	
Best Food Fast	£6.99		Just For Two	£6.99	
Breads & Muffins	£6.99		Kids' Birthday Cakes	£6.99	
Brunches, Lunches & Treats	£6.99		Kids Cooking	£6.99	
Cafe Classics	£6.99		Kids' Cooking Step-by-Step	£6.99	
Café Favourites	£6.99		Low-carb, Low-fat	£6.99	
Cakes Bakes & Desserts	£6.99		Low-fat Food for Life	£6.99	
Cakes Biscuits & Slices	£6.99		Low-fat Meals in Minutes	£6.99	
Cakes Cooking Class	£6.99		Main Course Salads	£6.99	
Caribbean Cooking	£6.99		Mexican	£6.99	
Casseroles	£6.99		Middle Eastern Cooking Class	£6.99	
Casseroles & Slow-Cooked Classics	£6.99		Mince in Minutes	£6.99	
Cheap Eats	£6.99		Moroccan & the Foods of North Africa	£6.99	
Cheesecakes: baked and chilled	£6.99		Muffins, Scones & Breads	£6.99	
Chicken	£6.99		New Casseroles	£6.99	
Chicken Meals in Minutes	£6.99		New Curries	£6.99	
Chinese and the foods of Thailand, Vietnam, Malaysia & Japan	£6.99		New Finger Food	£6.99	
			New French Food	£6.99	
Chinese Cooking Class	£6.99		New Salads	£6.99	
Christmas Cooking	£6.99		Party Food and Drink	£6.99	
Chocs & Treats	£6.99		Pasta Meals in Minutes	£6.99	
Cocktails	£6.99		Potatoes	£6.99	
Cookies & Biscuits	£6.99		Quick & Simple Cooking	£6.99	
Cooking Class Cake Decorating	£6.99		Rice & Risotto	£6.99	
Cupcakes & Fairycakes	£6.99		Sauces Salsas & Dressings	£6.99	
Detox	£6.99		Sensational Stir-Fries	£6.99	
Dinner Lamb	£6.99		Simple Healthy Meals	£6.99	
Easy Comfort Food	£6.99		Simple Starters Mains & Puds	£6.99	
Easy Curry	£6.99		Soup	£6.99	
Easy Midweek Meals	£6.99		Stir-fry	£6.99	
Easy Spanish-Style	£6.99		Superfoods for Exam Success	£6.99	
Food for Fit and Healthy Kids	£6.99		Tapas Mezze Antipasto & other bites	£6.99	
Foods of the Mediterranean	£6.99		Thai Cooking Class	£6.99	
Foods That Fight Back	£6.99		Traditional Italian	£6.99	
Fresh Food Fast	£6.99		Vegetarian Meals in Minutes	£6.99	
Fresh Food for Babies & Toddlers	£6.99		Vegie Food	£6.99	
Good Food for Babies & Toddlers	£6.99		Wicked Sweet Indulgences	£6.99	
Great Kids' Cakes	£6.99		Wok Meals in Minutes	£6.99	
Greek Cooking Class	£6.99		TOTAL COST:	£	

Mr/Mrs/Ms _____

Address _____ Postcode _____

Day time phone _____ email* (optional) _____

I enclose my cheque/money order for £ _____

or please charge £ _____

to my: ☐ Access ☐ Mastercard ☐ Visa ☐ Diners Club

Card number ☐☐☐☐ ☐☐☐☐ ☐☐☐☐ ☐☐☐☐

Expiry date _____ 3 digit security code *(found on reverse of card)* _____

Cardholder's name _____ Signature _____

To order: Mail or fax – photocopy or complete the order form above, and send your credit card details or cheque payable to: Australian Consolidated Press (UK), ACP Books, 10 Scirocco Close, Moulton Park Office Village, Northampton NN3 6AP. phone (+44) (0)1604 642200 fax (+44) (0)1604 642300 email books@acpuk.com or order online at www.acpuk.com
Non-UK residents: We accept the credit cards listed on the coupon, or cheques, drafts or International Money Orders payable in sterling and drawn on a UK bank. Credit card charges are at the exchange rate current at the time of payment. **Postage and packing UK:** Add £1.00 per order plus £1.75 per book. **Postage and packing overseas:** Add £2.00 per order plus £3.50 per book. All pricing current at time of going to press and subject to change/availability. **Offer ends 31.12.2008**

* By including your email address, you consent to receipt of any email regarding this magazine, and other emails which inform you of ACP's other publications, products, services and events, and to promote third party goods and services you may be interested in.

TEST KITCHEN
Food director Pamela Clark
Associate food editor Alexandra Somerville
Test Kitchen manager Kellie-Marie Thomas
Home economist Nancy Duran
Nutritional information Belinda Farlow

ACP BOOKS
General manager Christine Whiston
Editorial director Susan Tomnay
Creative director & designer Hieu Chi Nguyen
Senior editor Wendy Bryant
Director of sales Brian Cearnes
Marketing manager Bridget Cody
Business analyst Ashley Davies
Operations manager David Scotto
International rights enquires Laura Bamford
lbamford@acpuk.com

ACP Books are published by ACP Magazines
a division of PBL Media Pty Limited
Group publisher, Women's lifestyle Pat Ingram
Director of sales, Women's lifestyle Lynette Phillips
Commercial manager, Women's lifestyle Seymour Cohen
Marketing director, Women's lifestyle Matthew Dominello
Public relations manager, Women's lifestyle Hannah Deveraux
Creative director, Events, Women's lifestyle Luke Bonnano
Research Director, Women's lifestyle Justin Stone
ACP Magazines, Chief Executive officer Scott Lorson
PBL Media, Chief Executive officer Ian Law

Produced by ACP Books, Sydney.
Printed by Dai Nippon Printing in Korea.
Published by ACP Books, a division of
ACP Magazines Ltd, 54 Park St, Sydney;
GPO Box 4088, Sydney, NSW 2001.
Ph: (02) 9282 8618 Fax: (02) 9267 9438.
acpbooks@acpmagazines.com.au
www.acpbooks.com.au
Send recipe enquiries to:
recipeenquiries@acpmagazines.com.au

Australia Distributed by Network Services,
phone +61 2 9282 8777 fax +61 2 9264 3278
networkweb@networkservicescompany.com.au
United Kingdom Distributed by
Australian Consolidated Press (UK),
phone (01604) 642 200 fax (01604) 642 300
books@acpuk.com
New Zealand Distributed by Netlink
Distribution Company,
phone (9) 366 9966 ask@ndc.co.nz
South Africa Distributed by PSD Promotions,
phone (27 11) 392 6065/7
fax (27 11) 392 6079/80
orders@psdprom.co.za
Canada Distributed by Publishers Group Canada
phone (800) 663 5714 fax (800) 565 3770
service@raincoast.com

Quick and simple cooking: the Australian women's weekly
Includes index.
ISBN 978 1 86396 775 4 (pbk.).
1. Quick and easy cookery. I. Clark, Pamela.
II Title: Australian women's weekly
641.5
© ACP Magazines Ltd 2008
ABN 18 053 273 546

ACP Magazines Ltd Privacy Notice
This book may contain offers, competitions or surveys that require you to provide information about yourself if you choose to enter or take part in any such Reader Offer. If you provide information about yourself to ACP Magazines Ltd, the company will use this information to provide you with the products or services you have requested, and may supply your information to contractors that help ACP to do this. ACP will also use your information to inform you of other ACP publications, products, services and events. ACP will also give your information to organisations that are providing special prizes or offers, and that are clearly associated with the Reader Offer. Unless you tell us not to, we may give your information to other organisations that use it to inform you about other products, services and events or who may give it to other organisations that may use it for this purpose. If you would like to gain access to the information ACP holds about you, please contact ACP's Privacy Officer at ACP Magazines Ltd, 54-58 Park Street, Sydney, NSW 2000, Australia.

☐ **Privacy Notice** Please do not provide information about me to any organisation not associated with this offer.